Indirect Rule in South Africa

Rochester Studies in African History and the Diaspora

Toyin Falola, Senior Editor
The Frances Higginbotham Nalle Centennial Professor in History
University of Texas at Austin

(ISSN: 1092–5228)

A complete list of titles in the Rochester Studies in African History and the Diaspora, in order of publication, may be found at the end of this book.

Indirect Rule in South Africa

Tradition, Modernity, and the Costuming of Political Power

J. C. MYERS

UNIVERSITY OF ROCHESTER PRESS

First published 2008
Reprinted in paperback and transferred to digital printing 2013

University of Rochester Press
668 Mt. Hope Avenue, Rochester, NY 14620, USA
www.urpress.com
and Boydell & Brewer Limited
PO Box 9, Woodbridge, Suffolk IP12 3DF, UK
www.boydellandbrewer.com

ISSN: 1092–5228
hardcover ISBN: 978-1-58046-278-5
paperback ISBN: 978-1-58046-362-1

Library of Congress Cataloging-in-Publication Data

Myers, J. C.
    Indirect rule in South Africa : tradition, modernity, and the costuming of political
power / J. C. Myers.
    p. cm. — (Rochester studies in African history and the diaspora, ISSN 1092-5228 ;
v. 33)
Includes bibliographical references and index.
    ISBN-13: 978-1-58046-278-5 (hardcover : alk. paper)
    ISBN-10: 1-58046-278-2
    1. South Africa—Politics and government—1994– 2. Power (Social sciences)—
South Africa. I. Title.
    JQ1931.M94 2008
    320.968–dc22   2008000083

A catalogue record for this title is available from the British Library.

This publication is printed on acid-free paper.
Printed in the United States of America

Planning for segregation: from indirect rule to apartheid. "The Architects of Apartheid," Johnnic Media Collection, Museum Africa, Johannesburg

Contents

Preface

On March 21, 1960, a large crowd of demonstrators assembled outside the local police station in the segregated township of Sharpeville, South Africa. They had come to protest a recent tightening of the so-called pass laws requiring most South Africans to carry an identity document detailing their official race classification, residence, employment, and police records. The ratcheting up of the pass laws was a central element in the effort by the National Party (NP) to consolidate and strengthen the country's already thoroughgoing system of racial hierarchy. For those race-classified as "African" deference to the pass laws meant severe constriction of movement, residence rights, and employment, while violation of them meant risking arrest, deportation to a distant rural area, or a term of forced labor on a prison farm.

Eyewitnesses estimated the size of the crowd at between three and ten thousand.[1] Police reinforcements had arrived throughout the morning, and by early afternoon a line of officers armed with assault rifles stood between the protestors and the police station's fence. Without warning, the police opened fire. Sixty-nine people were killed and one hundred eighty wounded—most of them hit in the back as they fled.[2] Newspaper photographers had been on the scene and images of the massacre found their way into the international press, provoking levels of scrutiny, criticism, and sanction that South Africa's government had previously been spared. Foreign investors briefly withdrew from the country's economy and, for the first time, the United Nations General Assembly passed a resolution encouraging member states to take action against what the NP now referred to as apartheid.[3]

For the next three decades—from the 1976 Soweto riots to the popular insurgency of the 1980s, both periods backgrounded by the long imprisonment of Nelson Mandela, Walter Sisulu, Govan Mbeki, and other leaders of the antiapartheid movement—images of government-sponsored violence and coercion would continue to define the world's perception of South Africa. Yet, while a long line of segregationist governments in South Africa—stretching from British colonial authorities in the 1840s to the last defenders of apartheid in the late 1980s—rarely hesitated to use force in defense of their rule, they also struggled constantly for legitimacy. Their primary strategy in that struggle was *the costuming of political power,* the basic template for which was established by the British colonial policy of indirect rule. The co-opting of indigenous political authorities by imperialist officials has typically been understood as little more than an expedient solution to resource constraints: lacking sufficient numbers of their own personnel with which to establish local-level governance in colonized African territories, British authorities sought out the cooperation of tribal chiefs. It will be my argument here that the institutions of indirect rule represented much more. Rather than a field-expedient means of staffing local governments in rural areas, indirect rule was an ideological strategy, intended to legitimize the power of the colonial state.

This can be seen most clearly in the South African case by the fact that as the capacity of the state grew, the institutions of indirect rule were not eliminated, but elaborated and expanded. The ideas at the heart of indirect rule came to shape and define the projects of racial segregation and hierarchy in South Africa. They provided, also, the tactical framework with which authorities in the apartheid era attempted to defeat the insurgency that fought the NP government to a stalemate in the late 1980s. The connections between the colonial project of the 1840s and the urban battlefields of the 1980s have previously gone unrecognized. But in its deployment of township vigilante squads and false-front political parties, the apartheid state drew upon the same basic ideological strategy pioneered by indirect rule, contesting for legitimacy through the use of political proxies.

While the present study is concerned with tracing and explicating these connections, its primary focus will be on the institution of chieftaincy and its position in the ideological struggles for state legitimacy in South Africa. The narrowness of this focus is justified in two ways. First, South Africa's broad political development in the twentieth century was deeply tied to the institutions of indirect rule chieftaincy. Those institutions can be seen to have provided models on which several of the most critical aspects of South African segregation and apartheid were based. A second justification for the attention paid to chieftaincy in these pages can be found in the institution's unexpected survival at the beginning of the twenty-first century. While even relatively institutionalized apartheid-era political apparatuses such as the Bantustan system collapsed almost instantaneously at the moment of South Africa's transition to nonracial democracy, the powers and role of chieftaincy became first a heated point of debate and civil conflict, then a shaping force on the country's new constitution. As the transition began in the early 1990s, many of those who had functioned as chiefs came forward to demand a continued role in government. Their positions of power were warranted, they maintained, by their cultural status as "traditional leaders." The chiefs eventually won a protected place in the country's new constitution, albeit one bearing less in the way of political power than they had originally hoped to secure.

The study's central focus on the KwaZulu-Natal region is justified on similar grounds. It was here that the system of indirect rule was first introduced into South Africa and here that the more elaborate political innovations based on the models provided by indirect rule chieftaincy were developed and deployed. For reasons directly related to this fact, it was also in KwaZulu-Natal that the postapartheid conflict over the future status and role of chieftaincy became the most protracted and violent. It was in KwaZulu-Natal that a low-level civil war, thoroughly infused with the debate over chieftaincy, smoldered and occasionally flared for nearly a decade in the 1990s.

Proposing to examine a struggle for state legitimation will necessarily mean confronting at least some of the more prominent theories of legitimacy in the history of political thought. While I have drawn from such theories where they have proved useful, I have also endeavored to avoid their primary pitfall: functionalist assumptions, bordering on the tautological. All too often, political scientists have made the error of holding that the legitimacy of the King of X is evidenced by the fact that X is governed by monarchy. Rather than presuming that legitimacy must be a condition of governance and that, therefore, any existing system of government must be underpinned by a corresponding form of legitimacy, I have undertaken here to investigate the history of a strategy of legitimation. For this reason, theories of ideology have also proved useful in the course of my analysis, although these, too, have sometimes been hobbled by functionalist baggage. Louis Althusser's theory of ideology, for example, is particularly helpful in explaining the inner workings of the legitimation strategy employed by the colonial, segregationist, and apartheid states in South Africa.[4] I have made no attempt, however, to grapple with the metatheoretical implications of Althusser's contribution to the historical materialist tradition, nor have I accepted uncritically the functionalist implications of Althusser's work on ideology. Rather, it will be my argument that the evidence under examination here specifically denies such conclusions.

To the extent that the legitimation strategies described in this study were meant to preserve white supremacy in South Africa for all time, they must now be judged as having failed in their task. We may be tempted, in this sense, to regard them only as the curious relics of a peculiar regime. We would be mistaken in doing so. Both the institutional and ideological remnants of indirect rule shaped the trajectory of the postapartheid transition and continue to influence political life in South Africa. The story of that country's transition to democracy is incomplete without an account of the struggle over "traditional authority." But the particular nature of that struggle also allows for an unveiling of the ideological machinery at the heart of all forms of cultural legitimacy, from classic expressions of nationalism to contemporary forms of identity politics.

Throughout the debate over the question of a postapartheid political role for chieftaincy, the issue of the institution's legitimacy was frequently raised, though rarely investigated. Critics called for the chiefs' legitimacy to be tested by local elections in rural areas. The chiefs and their supporters countered that the cultural status of hereditary rule obviated the need for any sort of formal referendum. The debate appeared, at times, to be a clash of cultures: Western democracy's demand for government by the consent of the governed failing to comprehend an African cultural sanction for hereditary leadership. A large portion of this study's concern is with the extent to which this inaccurate and unhelpful dichotomy is supported by reified concepts of tradition and modernity. The case of indirect rule in South Africa reveals an entirely permeable boundary between the traditional and the modern, if a boundary can be said to exist at all. As competing concepts of legitimacy met one another in the debate over postapartheid chieftaincy, what was revealed was not the existence of two contrasting frames of reference, African and European, but the production of an illusory form of legitimacy by the institution of chieftaincy itself. The conclusions to be drawn from the South African struggle over the political role of chieftaincy, then, are of relevance to the investigation of a much broader question that has been of central concern to political philosophy since its origin in ancient times: To whom should political authority be granted and why should such authority be respected and obeyed?

A final note should be made with respect to the treatment in these pages of the concept of race. The thoroughgoing racialization of South African society since the onset of colonial rule has made it extremely cumbersome, if not virtually impossible, to discuss events in the country's political history while simultaneously maintaining a rigorously critical distance from racial terminology. My employment here of racial identifiers ("black," "white," "Native") is meant to correspond with the idiomatic usage of these terms in South Africa, not to signal an uncritical endorsement of any particular theory of race.

* * *

Sincere thanks go to all those who helped in innumerable ways to make this study possible, from the government officials and party representatives who granted me interviews, to the ordinary South Africans who made me welcome during my time there. Financial support was provided by the Rocca Memorial Fund, the Ford Foundation, the National Science Foundation, and California State University-Stanislaus. Special thanks go to Andrew Lawrence, Robert Price, Paul Thomas, Hanna Pitkin, Shannon Stimson, Michael Metelits, Gail Gerhart, John Daniel, Adam Habib, Sipho Sibanda, Rupert Taylor, Desmond Abrahams, Elroy Africa, Michael MacDonald, Toyin Falola, and Suzanne Guiod.

Abbreviations

AEC	Adult Education Consultants / Eduguide
ANC	African National Congress
AWB	Afrikaner Resistance Movement
AZAPO	Azanian People's Organization
BOSS	Bureau of State Security
CODESA	Convention for a Democratic South Africa
CONTRALESA	Congress of Traditional Leaders of South Africa
COSATU	Congress of South African Trade Unions
CP	Conservative Party
FRELIMO	Front for the Liberation of Mozambique
IFP	Inkatha Freedom Party
ISA	ideological state apparatus
KLA	KwaZulu Legislative Assembly
MDM	Mass Democratic Movement
NAD	Native Affairs Department
NHTL	National House of Traditional Leaders
NP	National Party
NRC	Natives Representatives Council
PAC	Pan-Africanist Congress
RENAMO	Mozambican National Resistance
RSA	repressive state apparatus
SACP	South African Communist Party
SADF	South African Defence Force
SANCO	South African National Civic Organization
SAP	South African Police
SASO	South African Students' Organization
SATHCO	South African Traditional Healers' Council
SSC	State Security Council
SSRC	Soweto Student Representatives Council
SWAPO	South West African People's Organization

UDF	United Democratic Front
UNITA	National Union for the Total Independence of Angola
UTTGC	United Transkeian Territories General Council
UWUSA	United Workers Union of South Africa

1

Indirect Rule

In the summer of 1957, at the British Colonial Office's Conference on African Administration, a working group convened to discuss "the place of chiefs in African administration" reported their finding that "the brilliant classical period of indirect rule is over."[1] With independence movements now sweeping the continent and the decolonization of Africa in full swing, the Colonial Office put its best face forward, declaring (if already a bit nostalgically) the successful tenure of a form of governance that had become its hallmark.

The origins of indirect rule can be traced back at least as far as the 1850s in the thinking of colonial administrators in India and Natal, though its best-known application and elaboration was in the administration of Northern Nigeria under Frederick Lugard in the early 1900s. Its basic premise was simple: rather than building from the ground up wholly new forms of government in colonized territories, British sovereignty would be layered atop existing indigenous institutions. African elites would continue to rule over the day-to-day affairs of a subject population, though always under the final oversight of the colonial governor.

In his study of the system of indirect rule, Mahmood Mamdani argues that the analysis of this peculiar form of state permits the development of what might be called a unified theory of colonialism in sub-Saharan Africa.[2] Where previous generations of scholarship had suggested a sharp differentiation in economic and political development separating South Africa from the rest of the continent, Mamdani's theory proposes a model capable of accounting for colonial rule and its aftermath on both sides of the Limpopo. Yet, in his struggle to emphasize the commonalities in colonial experiences across the African continent, Mamdani loses sight of some crucial distinctions. In particular, the political requirements of South Africa's large population of permanent settlers differed from those of the administrative regimes in Nigeria or the Gold Coast. For example, Mamdani describes indirect rule as a form of decentralized despotism,[3] yet in South Africa indirect rule was not aimed simply at the development or operation of blunt, brute tyranny. Instead, what characterized the system of indirect rule as it was assembled and elaborated in South Africa was its central position in a strategy designed to build legitimacy for the colonial and segregationist states.

Political Expediency

The most frequently proposed hypothesis explaining the development of indirect rule focuses on the demands of colonial competition and the scarcity of resources with which to fulfill them. Colonial administration is, in most cases, an expensive, high-risk undertaking, more comparable to military invasion than to normal governance. Yet, in the European partition of sub-Saharan Africa, the pressures inherent to colonial rule were dramatically intensified by the formal requirements of the partition itself and the highly competitive environment they gave rise to. By establishing "effective occupation" (a basic military presence and a skeletal administrative capacity) as the criterion by which European states would recognize one another's claims to African territories, the 1884 Berlin Conference is commonly understood to have made the system of indirect rule a virtual necessity.[4] In this view, the administrators directly responsible for the real business of colonization—racing for a foothold on the newly opened continent and facing shortages of personnel and equipment—are argued to have made use of the political resources most directly at hand: the chiefs already occupying seats of power in African societies.

That chiefs did, in fact, occupy positions of power in sub-Saharan African societies was an assumption British colonists carried with them from the first days of the partition. The anthropological model upon which they depended was one suggesting that clear lines of political authority ran from kings through chiefs to households.[5] The reality on the ground proved to be far more complex. Some societies, it turned out, had no specialized elites who fit the prevailing anthropological concept of a chief.[6] In such cases, where British authorities could not find what they were looking for ready-made, they chose to manufacture it—creating a chieftaincy where none had existed before. In other instances, where hereditary elites actually appeared to exist, deeper problems arose. Here, the difficulty was not in locating a chief, but in controlling the institution of chieftaincy. A leader whose position was sanctioned by local custom but who rebelled against colonial policy could hardly be allowed to remain in a position of power. Thus, the continued application of indirect rule over long periods of time required the colonial state to assume final responsibility for the appointment and deposition of chiefs and to continually break and recreate the chains of hereditary succession. Distilling this convoluted mixture of history, anthropology, and bureaucratic formality into an operational concept, the British Colonial Office defined the term "chief" to include "nontraditional chiefs appointed in terms of a law of the territory concerned and also traditional chiefs formally 'recognized' as chiefs required by a law," but excluded "persons sometimes known as chiefs but not statutorily appointed or recognized."[7]

The manufacturing and manipulation of chieftaincy began in the late 1840s, in the British colony of Natal. The creator of sub-Saharan Africa's first system of indirect rule, Theophilus Shepstone (the British government's "Diplomatic Agent to the Native Tribes"), has often been described as having placed a layer of British colonial administration over the preexisting institutions of African chieftaincy.[8] Yet, even Edgar Brookes, an advisor to National Party leader and staunch segregationist J. B. Hertzog, admitted that upon taking office in 1846, Shepstone was faced not with the task of reining in a system of indigenous political authority where it remained vibrant, but of artificially recreating one where it had disappeared.[9] The persons under Shepstone's jurisdiction in Natal were largely refugees of the *Mfecane*—the violent consolidation of the Zulu state under Shaka in the 1820s—and Shepstone himself estimated that more than two-thirds of this population no longer lived under any form of chieftaincy.[10] The transformative rather than preservative nature of indirect rule is evident in the fact that its application to Zululand—the territory north of the colony's original borders—came only after the military defeat of the Zulu state, the dismantling of the existing system of chieftaincy, and the appointment of new chiefs presiding over officially demarcated territories.[11]

The transformation of economic life brought about through the institutions and practices of indirect rule is particularly striking. A hut tax, collected by chiefs, was introduced to Natal in 1848. After its extension to Zululand in the 1880s, the tax accounted for over 70 percent of the colony's total revenue.[12] After 1848, forced labor was also drawn through chiefs, who were required to provide the state with one laborer for every eleven huts falling under their jurisdiction.[13] For those identified as "Natives," a connection was thereby established between subject and state, mediated by the figure of the chief, whose purpose was the designation of roles in the economic sphere. To be identified by the state as a Native meant, simultaneously, to be determined as a specific agent of production. The state made no such determination for those in Natal identified as non-Natives or "Europeans." Within the whole of its domain, then, the colonial state took on both capitalist and precapitalist aspects, arranged along a racial divide.[14] The "tribal society" presided over by chieftaincy was meant to remain as a precapitalist enclave within the larger framework of a developing capitalism, but only in a very specific and limited sense: it was intended to retain the identifying features of precolonial society while its contents were radically altered.

One example of this dynamic can be seen in the treatment by colonial authorities of the practice of *lobolo* (the exchange of cattle between families as a form of bride-price). During the codification of customary law in Natal, colonial authorities interpreted *lobolo* as a type of commercial transaction, rather than as a reciprocal social obligation. As maximum *lobolo* charges were set, the families of brides-to-be began routinely to demand the maximum number of cattle. Young men seeking to marry thus discovered in the codification of custom an entirely new pressure driving them into the labor market.[15]

A further example can be recognized in the system of communal land tenure, frequently referred to as one of the key elements of precolonial society that had been preserved by the policy of segregated landholding.[16] In precolonial chieftaincies, land was allocated by a chief to members of a community who maintained rights of use and occupation, but not of ownership.[17] Under indirect rule, the allocation of land for cultivation remained within the purview of a chief, but set within the wider framework of colonial society, its institutional content and material importance were dramatically transformed. The general (though not unlimited) availability of land prior to colonial rule left open the possibility for members of a community presided over by a chief to break ranks and strike out on their own. Though the advantages of social membership would clearly have been significant (clearing of land, social accumulation of resources to withstand drought or crop failure), they did not amount to the ability of a chief to have boundless authority over his subjects. The demarcation of Native reserves within which chiefs allocated subsistence plots now curtailed the ability of subjects to check the power of a chief through desertion. As Mamdani suggests, the inclusion of land allocation within the scope of chiefly authority "provided the basis of a political despotism."[18] This is the very moment described by Rousseau in "Discourse on the Origins of Inequality" in which the nonconsensual relations of both chattel and wage slavery become possible:

> A man could well lay hold of the fruit another has gathered, the game he has killed, the cave that served as his shelter. But how will he ever succeed in making himself obeyed? And what can be the chains of dependence among men who possess nothing? If someone chases me from one tree, I am free to go to another; If someone torments me in one place, who will prevent me from going elsewhere?[19]

Yet, as powerful as coercive force may appear in the short run or in the particular case of a confrontation between lone individual and state apparatus, in the long run or in the relationship between state apparatus and mass population, it is never enough.

The problems posed by the limits of coercion are amplified in the case of indirect rule by the unusual amount of effort British authorities devoted to creating and maintaining the institutions of chieftaincy. If, as the long-standing explanations of indirect rule propose, co-opting African elites was simply the most efficient solution to the problem of colonial governance, it is not clear why chieftaincies—rather than some other form of government—were created in societies that had no such institution or recreated in societies whose systems of chieftaincy had either disappeared or been intentionally destroyed. More importantly, the shortage of resources facing colonial administrators in the early days of the partition fails to explain the sustained preference for chieftaincy over time. Why, as greater levels of resources became available, were modern European forms of government not developed to replace the supposed stopgap solution of indirect rule? Similar questions might be asked of Mamdani's suggestion that indirect rule chieftaincy represented a form of decentralized despotism. If the colonial state sought only (or even primarily) the application of coercive force, why place the task in the hands of chiefs?

Legitimacy and Interpellation

Every form of state must win the obedience of its subjects or perish. For the colonial state—a foreign occupier, operating at a great distance from its centers of power and in the midst of an unfamiliar culture—that imperative could not have been more pointed. The basket loads of severed hands, taken from the victims of Belgium's "Bula Matari" state in the Congo, remain one of the more lurid reminders of the extent to which the colonization of sub-Saharan Africa depended upon the application of coercive force.[20] Yet, wherever the colonial state sought to endure over the long run, it also sought to legitimate itself in the eyes of its subject population. The reasons why this was the case take us to the very heart of political theory. Every thinker concerned with state power has ultimately been driven to confront the concept of legitimacy.

No better explication of this axiom is available to us than Niccolo Machiavelli's landmark discourse on state power, *The Prince*. Incautious readers of the Florentine diplomat's text have for ages come away with the lesson that in politics, the ends justify the means: any tool or technique that serves to maximize the power of the state is an acceptable one to employ, provided only that it works. A more thorough examination of *The Prince* reveals that Machiavelli was far more concerned with explaining *which* tools and techniques tend to succeed at maximizing state power than with offering a justification for their use. Consider, for example, his infamous answer to the question of whether it is better for a leader to be feared or loved. On the one hand, the brute efficacy of fear and the capriciousness of love lead Machiavelli to conclude that if it is not possible to sustain both, a leader should prefer to be feared.[21] On the other hand, he constantly warns throughout the text that a leader must, above all, avoid being hated. Why should a leader capable of instilling fear in the hearts of his subjects himself fear hatred? Because even coercive force has its limits:

> So it should be noted that when he seizes a state the new ruler must determine all the injuries that he will need to inflict. He must inflict them once for all, and not have to renew them every day, and in that way he will be able to set men's minds at rest and win them over to him when he confers benefits. Whoever acts otherwise, either through timidity or misjudgment, is always forced to have the knife ready in his hand and can never depend on his subjects because they, suffering fresh and continuous violence, can never feel secure with regard to him.[22]

Brutality may be an effective measure against small numbers of dissidents, criminals, or insurgents who either ignore or resist the law, but should a majority turn angrily against the state, arms alone are unlikely to save it.[23]

It is this point that allows us to understand why, after concurring with Trotsky that, "every state is founded on force," Max Weber went on to detail not the application of force, but the ways in which state power was made legitimate.[24] In *The Theory of Social and Economic Organization*, he offered what we shall take here to be a provisional description of legitimacy:

> In general, it should be kept clearly in mind that the basis of every system of authority, and correspondingly of every kind of willingness to obey, is a belief, a belief by virtue of which persons exercising authority are lent prestige.[25]

We need not yet agree with Weber that every state, or every system of authority, is in fact upheld by a condition of belief, though it is clear to see why such a condition would be of tremendous value to political leaders. It is surely possible to compel people to work or to fight, to pay taxes or to keep silent through the use or the threat of force. Slaves faced with torture or death for noncompliance have mined precious metals, grown cotton, even assembled long-range ballistic missiles. Yet, the Nazi V-2 factories would seem to represent a historical anomaly. Slave production is typically carried out with only the most basic hand tools, precisely because the possibility for sabotage is so great. Obedience, in other words, may be had through the use of force, but it is sure to be highly inefficient. People driven to work by whips are likely to do only what they must to avoid punishment and can be expected to remain constantly on the lookout for opportunities to rebel. Moreover, the resources necessary for the application of coercive force are not cheap. Each soldier needed to oversee a productive worker is an unproductive mouth needing to be fed. And, unless the soldiers guarding the slaves are themselves to be guarded by other guards, ad infinitum, even a highly coercive system of power would require a substantial layer of believers.

How, then, might a cadre—or better still, a population—of believers be assembled? Machiavelli's advice regarding the organization of effective military forces is instructive here. Mercenaries he roundly rejects, maintaining that the receipt of a fee is hopelessly insufficient to create the type of loyalty that will inspire soldiers to die for their commanders in the field.[26] Instead, he counsels the creation of a citizen militia:

> Now, no new prince has ever at any time disarmed his subjects; rather, when he has found them unarmed he has always given them arms. This is because by arming your subjects you arm yourself; those who were suspect become loyal, and those who were loyal not only remain so but are changed from being merely your subjects to being your partisans.[27]

It is not, of course, the transfer of arms per se that changes subject into partisan, so much as the message of trust and common interest communicated by the exchange. The prince who arms his subjects creates not simply an army, but a common form of identity enfolding both leaders and led. Machiavelli's image here is of a soldier who faces death not for the sake of some distant abstraction, but for a community in which he perceives himself to be a member.

While Weber's concept of legitimacy differs in its suggestion of a historical trajectory of political transformation stretching from the small-scale society to industrial modernity, it too would seem to root legitimate authority in a shared sense of identity. On the one hand, Weber's work (and that of the generation of post–World War II scholars reared on his texts) gives particular emphasis to the distinctions drawn between three basic forms of legitimacy. Tradition finds the stamp of approval bestowed upon the practices of the past; the "eternal yesterday." Charisma denotes the extraordinary personal magnetism of the revolutionary leader or the demagogue. Rational-legality contrasts these with "the belief in the validity of legal statute."[28] On the other hand, the viability of each distinct form of Weberian legitimacy hinges on a common requirement. The eternal yesterday, for example, does not refer to a radically unbounded past, encompassing all of humanity. In order for me to know that a particular tradition establishes a legitimate precedent for me to respect and obey, I must have some means of distinguishing it from the range of other such traditions, based in different remembrances of the past. The charismatic leader, too, is surely only one of many voices calling for my attention in the public square. What his extraordinary magnetism sets into motion is a unique field of attraction between his person and mine. Even belief in the validity of legal statute is not a belief that *all* legal statutes are equally binding upon me, but the belief that certain laws (those made by a government I recognize to be my own) must be complied with, while others (those enacted by foreign states) can be safely ignored.

Thus, although Weber describes for us at least three external forms that the process of legitimation takes, he stops short of explaining the inner workings of that process: the establishment of a privileged line of communication between those who command and those who obey. This work was left to Louis Althusser, in his landmark essay on ideology. Working from within the historical materialist tradition, Althusser reframes Weber's opening question concerning legitimacy ("When and why do men obey? Upon what inner justifications and upon what external means does this domination rest?"[29]), setting it within the context of a broader inquiry into the nature of the social relations of production.[30] In doing so, however, he simultaneously suggests a powerful critique of the once dominant interpretation of historical materialist theory, which found its inspiration in the 1859 preface to Marx's *Contribution to the Critique of Political Economy*:

> In the social production of their existence, men enter into definite relations that are indispensable and independent of their will, relations of production which correspond to a definite stage of development of their material productive forces. . . . At a certain stage of their development, the material productive forces of society come in conflict with the existing relations of production, or—what is but a legal expression for the same thing—with the property relations within which they have been at work hitherto. From forms of development of the productive forces these relations turn into their fetters. Then begins an epoch of social revolution. With the change of the economic foundation the entire immense superstructure is more or less rapidly transformed.[31]

As G. A. Cohen argues in his interpretation of this school of historical materialism, the line of determination (and, therefore, also of explanation) runs from productive forces to social relations. First come innovations in technologies and techniques, then, as a result, relationships of ownership and control are reconfigured.[32]

Often during the twentieth century, this version of historical materialist theory tended to give rise to a mechanistic, almost apolitical understanding of historical change. If social revolution was geared to the timetable of technological innovation, what role did political activity, leadership, or even sheer accident play in the transformation of human societies? Reflecting on these problems, some scholars returned to the opening section of the *Communist Manifesto*, in which Marx and Engels appeared to begin their analysis not from the level of development of the productive forces, but from the tensions and conflicts arising within the social relations of production:

> The history of all society up to now is the history of class struggles. Freeman and slave, patrician and plebeian, lord and serf, guild-master and journeyman, in short, oppressor and oppressed stood in continual conflict with one another,

conducting an unbroken, now hidden, now open struggle, a struggle that finished each time with a revolutionary transformation of society as a whole, or with the common ruin of the contending classes.[33]

As George Comninel argued in his study of the French Revolution, the explanatory framework of historical materialism properly centered itself on the antagonism and struggle between those directly responsible for the production of social surpluses and those capable of extracting and expropriating surplus goods.[34] In this reading of historical materialism, history was made by the gritty clashes of class struggle, not the steady ticking-over of technological improvement.

Considerable attention has been focused on the rift between these two competing accounts of historical materialism, yet one point of common ground between them is too frequently overlooked. As Cohen notes, revolutions transform relations of production, not productive forces.[35] This can only be the case, though, if a given set of productive forces corresponds with or creates the possibility for more than one set of productive relations. The number of possibilities clearly cannot be infinite. Electric motors and high-tensile steel correspond with the relations of factory production in a way that stone tools and human or animal-powered machines simply do not. Nonetheless, a general survey of industrial economies in the twentieth century would quickly attest to the fact that electric motors and high-tensile steel might correspond with a range of productive relations stretching from laissez-faire capitalism to centrally planned socialism, with various mixed models in between. Once the level of development of the productive forces has determined the scope of the technologically feasible, political struggles would be aimed at shaping and reshaping productive relations. It is within the context of this process, Althusser suggests, that we must search for an answer to Weber's question about obedience.

Althusser's restatement of that question, then, focuses attention on the reproduction of a society's conditions of production:

> I shall say that the reproduction of labour power requires not only a reproduction of its skills, but also, at the same time, a reproduction of its submission to the rules of the established order, i.e. a reproduction of submission to the ruling ideology for the workers, and a reproduction of the ability to manipulate the ruling ideology correctly for the agents of exploitation and repression, so that they, too, will provide for the domination of the ruling class "in words."[36]

We can recognize here a dual function served by ideology. First, the existing relations of production must be reproduced. Concrete human beings must be told—with greater or lesser specificity, depending upon the nature of the mode of production—what is expected of them; what they must and must not do.[37] Certain types of elites and certain modes of domination (to trans-late back into Weber's terms) must be justified and made legitimate. Second, because the forces of production do not mechanistically dictate the relations of production, a transformation of the exiting relations of production must be guarded against. Political actors of all kinds must be brought to believe that alternative forms of social life are either unrealistic or illegitimate. In this sense, ideology is understood to be an instrument of class struggle.[38]

Althusser's essay takes a significant step forward from this initial theoriza-tion of ideology (and opens the way for an empirical research agenda) by suggesting that ideology has a material existence, consisting of practices and rituals embedded in institutions.[39] The list of these ideological state appara-tuses (ISAs) is extensive, incorporating the fields of religion, education, pol-itics, media, and culture.[40] Three important points, however, can be extracted from this initial list. First, a distinction has been drawn between a plurality of ISAs and the singular repressive state apparatus (RSA): the sys-tem of armed forces, police, courts, and prisons. The former, Althusser argues, function mainly through ideology, while the latter operate mainly through violence.[41] Second, the specific forms taken by ISAs are subject to historical change. Whereas the church was once the dominant ISA in Western Europe, for example, it was gradually replaced by the public school.[42] Third, while the forms taken by ISAs are historically variable, their deep structure—the fundamental operation that makes them work—does not change; it is eternal to human history. ISAs always and everywhere inter-pellate persons as subjects.[43]

As Terry Eagleton has argued, this way of understanding the function of ideology is heavily indebted to Jacques Lacan's concept of the mirror stage, in which the infant's (mis)recognition of its mirror image as *itself* provides an imaginary (albeit necessary) platform from which to act in the world.[44] The mirror, it seems, contains a crucial flaw: where the concrete human being is irrational and contradictory, the mirror image is stable and coher-ent; where the real person is hopelessly torn by conflicting desires, the imag-inary self easily tells right from wrong. In much the same way, for Althusser, "ideology represents the imaginary relationship of individuals to their real conditions of existence."[45] Ideology, in other words, stitches together a com-prehensible narrative out of a complicated and contradictory world, explain-ing both the nature of that world and our particular place in it.

Yet, while the Lacanian self owes its birth to a specular mechanism, ideol-ogy, Althusser suggests, is doubly speculary:

> Which means that all ideology is *centered*, that the Absolute Subject occupies the unique place of the Centre, and interpellates around it the infinity of individuals into subjects in a double mirror-connexion such that it *subjects* the subjects to the Subject, while giving them in the Subject in which each subject

can contemplate its own image (present and future) the *guarantee* that this really concerns them.[46]

The ideological apparatus creates subjects in both senses of the word. Reflecting particular images of the concrete persons who gaze into it, ideology defines the (grammatical) subjects' range of action and possibility: what they are capable of doing, what they must and must not do, etc. Simultaneously, ideology produces (political) subjects: members of a hierarchy whose key position is occupied by an Absolute Subject. Most importantly, though, ideology establishes a relationship of identity between ordinary subjects and the Absolute Subject. It is this relationship that explains legitimacy's privileged line of communication: the subject's ability to recognize a particular leader or law as his own.[47] It is this relationship that the institutions of indirect rule were designed to establish between rural South Africans and the segregationist state.

Tradition and the Tribe

We can begin to recognize the role played by indirect rule chieftaincy in state legitimation through a careful examination of its inner workings, beginning with its core institution: the dual legal structure. Following the British annexation of Natal in 1843, Roman-Dutch law was applied to the population of the colony as a whole, without regard to racial classifications. By 1848, however, a debate had emerged within the colonial administration over the future of Natal's legal system. Dr. Henry Cloete, recorder for the Natal colonial government, argued in favor of maintaining the unitary system of Roman-Dutch law across the colony as a whole. He was opposed by Theophilus Shepstone, who favored the creation of a bifurcated system in which the settler population would be governed by Roman-Dutch law, while those designated as Natives would live under a codified system of customary law.[48] Shepstone prevailed and the dual legal structure was brought into existence by Ordinance 3 of 1849, though the rigorous codification of customary law did not begin until 1875, ultimately resulting in the Natal Native Code of 1891.

The recognition of customary law was limited, however, "in so far as it was not repugnant to the general principles of humanity observed throughout the civilized world."[49] This qualified application of customary law was duplicated in the Transvaal Republic by Law 4 of 1885, and in the British colonies of Kenya, Malawi, Southern Rhodesia, Ghana, Nigeria, Sierra Leone, and Sudan. In each instance, the validity of customary law was limited by permitting it to be tested against "natural justice," "public policy," or "humanity."[50] As with the invention of chieftaincy in previously stateless societies, the repugnancy clause in colonial legal systems serves to reveal the extent to which systems of indirect rule modified and manufactured indigenous political practices, while claiming only to recognize or reinstate them. On its surface, the existence of two systems of law and governance—one for "Natives" and one for "Europeans"—would appear to support the claim that institutions were being made to fit the reality on the ground: two distinct groups of people two distinct sets of laws and political institutions, appropriate to each one. Brookes, for example, writes of the re-creation of chieftaincy under indirect rule: "The system is perfectly understood by the Natives, carrying with it mutual responsibility and suretyship and requiring implicit obedience to authority."[51] Upon closer inspection, it becomes clear that precisely the reverse was true. Having established the dual legal structure at the outset of the colonial project, concrete persons would now have to be made to fit within it. As one South African jurist wrote in 1908:

> Obviously there has been extreme difficulty in finding a definition applicable to persons very unlike, with different degrees of culture, intelligence and civilization—a definition which will take account of racial inter-mixtures as well as degrees of culture. The lines of colour and those of culture do not necessarily, or in fact, coincide. The existence of these differences and the consequent uncertainty as to the legal position of many persons have brought evil with them. A large number of persons, and some of those most inclined to adopt civilized life, are left in an ambiguous position.[52]

As bodies of law and apparatuses of governance were applied to both individuals and communities, concrete persons were compelled to become "Native" or "European." Laws regarding landholding, marriage, even daily movement between rural and urban areas, established practices that gave life to the categories themselves. To the question, "Who am I?" the law provided definitive answers.

In the nature of the dual legal structure, then, we have at least one piece of evidence to suggest that at the heart of the system of indirect rule lay a material institution responsible for the interpellation of persons as subjects. Two problems, however, would seem to remain for the ISA thesis. First, while the dual legal structure does seem to have created forms of subjectivity for concrete persons, it is not yet clear that this task was accomplished by means of a specular mechanism. Second, if interpellation was carried out primarily via the legal system, this would seem to grant responsibility for it to what Althusser defines as the RSA, rather than the ISAs. But although the dual legal structure played a central role in the system of indirect rule, it formed only the nucleus of that system and, in a sense, the final stopping-point for challenges to the system. The ordinary work of interpellating subjects was to be carried out elsewhere.[53]

A clue as to the location of those ideological operations can be found in the 1903–5 debates over the specific form that racial hierarchy would take as British colonial possessions and Afrikaner republics were welded together to form the Union of South Africa. Louis Botha (the union's first prime minister) strongly opposed the replication of Natal's system of indirect rule in the rest of South Africa, arguing that the division of the country between Native and European areas would keep black labor away from the white-owned farms on which it was needed.[54] For Botha, a black working class was an inseparable—albeit unequal—component of the South African settler society, whose hierarchy would be reproduced using nothing more than the state's basic repressive machinery. Black workers would toil for white employers and, should a challenge ever arise, one side would have a ready supply of guns and ammunition, while the other would not.

A radically different vision of South Africa's future was presented in an address given before the British Association in 1905 by J. Howard Pim, a former employee of Cecil Rhodes's British South Africa Company and a member of the Johannesburg Town Council:

> For a time the location consists of able-bodied people, but they grow older, they become ill, they become disabled—who is to support them? They commit offenses—who is to control them? The reserve is a sanatorium where they can recruit; if they are disabled they remain there. Their own tribal system keeps them under discipline, and if they become criminals there is not the slightest difficulty in bringing them to justice. All this absolutely without cost to the white community.[55]

Here, Pim appears keenly aware of two crucial aspects of indirect rule that seem to have eluded Botha. First, segregation's form is distinguishable from its content. Botha's opposition to the extension of indirect rule was rooted in the assumption that segregation would perform according to its billing, removing blacks from white society and expelling their labor power with them. Yet, the tribal system in colonial Natal was no more an independent social formation than customary law was a separate, freestanding legal structure. Just as the repugnancy clause reveals the subsumption of customary within colonial law, the migratory labor system makes plain the operation of a single, undivided economy. With their wives, children, and elderly parents left behind in the reserves, the able-bodied men would be recruited out for work in the mines and on the farms. Second, the tribal system would function as a form of legitimate authority over its inmates, reducing or even eliminating the need for expensive deployments of coercive power. The Natives might be kept in line with ease and at low cost, if they could be persuaded that the rules to be obeyed had not been imposed by an alien power, but were the codes and customs of their own unique society.

The ideological functions of indirect rule are brought to the surface in the writings of one of the more influential figures surrounding the segregation debate, G. N. Heaton Nicholls, a Natal plantation owner and member of the Native Affairs Commission in the 1920s.[56] Nicholls, like Pim, argued for the adoption of a reserve system in the union as a whole, but was particularly interested in the possibilities a segregationist strategy seemed to offer for countering the looming spectre of proletarian politics:

> An adaptationist policy demands as its primary concept the maintenance of chieftaindom without which the tribal society cannot exist. . . . The adaptionist [*sic*] policy assumes a difference between the Abantu and the Europeans. It assumes some measure of territorial segregation. It assumes what in effect is the growth of a national consciousness amongst the Abantu themselves. . . . The opposite policy of assimilation substitutes class for race and if continued on its present basis must lead to the evolution of a native proletariat, inspired by the antagonisms of class war.[57]

Nicholls's commentary on segregation is notable for its betrayal of both an ideology of race (i.e., a concept of racial phenotypes as corresponding with particular social regimes) and the consciousness of an ideological strategy of racialization. In proposing the reconstruction of tribal communalism as the only means by which communism could be held off, Nicholls asks, in effect: Which would we prefer to live with, a black proletariat or a Bantu nation? Most strikingly, though, the question is not posed as one of description or even foretelling, but of production. Nicholls calls upon the state to take an active role in sustaining and fortifying the institutions of tribal society, thereby preventing the rise of some new and threatening social form. Of course, his suggestion here is not, as Louis Botha feared, that the objective, material nature of the developing proletariat should be altered; that the black working class be provided with sufficient land and capital and allowed to remove itself from South African agricultural and industrial production. What Nicholls suggests is a sort of costuming; a dressing-up of the black proletariat as a Bantu nation.

The requisite knowledge for such an operation would be provided by the developing field of anthropology. On his appointment to the newly established chair of social anthropology at the University of Cape Town in 1921, A. R. Radcliffe-Brown spoke of his science as a means for grasping the essential nature of human cultures, which might then be offered up to the guiding hands of the state. Writing in the journal *Bantu Studies*, launched the same year as his appointment, he argued that on the African continent,

> social anthropology is a subject not of merely scientific or academic interest, but of immense practical importance. The one great problem on which the future welfare of South Africa depends is that of finding some social and political system in which the natives and the whites may live together without conflict; and the successful solution of that problem would certainly seem to require a thorough knowledge of the native civilization between which and our own we need to establish some sort of harmonious relation.[58]

That harmonious relation, though, would be one modeled on the institutions of indirect rule, rather than on those of international relations: a modified version of the native civilization would be constructed within a segregated enclave of South African society. Anthropology would provide the necessary assemblage of cultural categories and the outlines of their corresponding social and political institutions. As if in response to Radcliffe-Brown's offer of anthropology's services, in 1925, the Native Affairs Department created an ethnological section, and in the following year, an award of £50 was offered to department officers who obtained a diploma in Bantu Studies or passed equivalent examinations.[59]

These special cadres of state ethnologists would be charged with producing the concepts of racial difference upon which a fully elaborated system of indirect rule could be based. Languages would be analyzed, customs would be catalogued, genealogies would be logged, all in the service of a form of segregation based not on distance, but on difference:

> There is only one way out . . . the path of differential development, the course dictated by that true liberalism which has ever stood for the preservation of small nationalities, the course dictated by that wise conservatism which is not prepared to sacrifice national institutions and natural divisions for an unknown and fear-inspiring future. For the preservation and happiness of white and black alike, we stand for the policy of differentiation.[60]

Difference, however, was valuable to the segregationist state only to the extent that it held out the promise of securing its political power. If the Natives would respect authority, provided that it appeared in a form prescribed by their unique society and culture (as a fundamentally Weberian understanding of legitimacy seemed to suggest), the ethnographic analysis of cultural difference would be a necessary prerequisite to the process of producing appropriately costumed authority figures.

By the early 1920s, then, far from preparing to eliminate the institutions of indirect rule in favor of modern European governmental structures, South Africa's segregationist leaders stood ready to elaborate and expand them. Through the remainder of the twentieth century, governments in South Africa would attempt to legitimize a strict and exploitative racial hierarchy through the use of an ideological strategy pioneered by British colonists in Natal. In this sense, Mamdani's suggestion that the outlines of the modern system of apartheid can be seen in the divided world of indirect rule is entirely correct. Yet, the structures of indirect rule were not simply barriers, designed to enforce the system of segregation, but ideological apparatuses, designed to legitimize it.

2

From Native Administration to Separate Development

The extension of chieftaincy's legal foundation during the 1920s makes clear the presumption on the part of South Africa's segregationist leaders that indirect rule was far more than a temporary colonial expedient. Yet, during the first half of the twentieth century, as the forces of modernity increasingly transformed the whole of South African society, the institutions of indirect rule came under mounting pressure. As industrialization drove the relocation of workers from rural villages to urban townships and industrial sites, even heavily modified versions of tribal social organization were strained to the breaking point. As electoral democracy gradually shifted its international status from radical working class demand to accepted bourgeois practice, both government officials and popular opposition leaders began to question the maintenance of hereditary chieftaincy. By the middle 1940s, South Africa seemed to face a critical juncture. One path led toward modernization and deracialization; another toward the desperate defense of segregation and the reinvigoration of indirect rule.

Elaboration and Expansion

The segregationist strategy of "differentiation" became law with the passage of the 1927 Native Administration Act. Under the act, the category of "Native" was defined to include, "any person who is a member of any aboriginal race or tribe of Africa," though as in other applications of indirect rule and customary law, the state retained the ability to exempt a person legally defined as a Native from "the laws specially affecting Natives."[1] The act applied key facets of the Natal Code of Native Law to the Union of South Africa as a whole and borrowed from the Natal Code its principle ideological innovation, the costuming of the governor-general as "supreme chief." In addition to his ordinary powers as an executive within the modern state, as supreme chief, the governor-general would be endowed with all the powers, authorities, functions, rights, immunities and privileges which according to the laws, customs and usages of Natives are exercised and enjoyed by any Supreme or Paramount Native Chief and which shall be deemed *inter alia* to include the following: (a) Power to call upon chiefs personally to render military or other service and to supply armed men or levies for the suppression of disorder or rebellion; (b) Authority in the exercise of his functions and powers to punish disobedience of his orders or disregard of his authority by fine or imprisonment or by both fine and imprisonment; (c) The function of Upper Guardian of all Native orphans and minors in law.[2]

In his supreme chief mask, the governor-general could make law by proclamation, divide, amalgamate, or create new tribes, and appoint or depose other chiefs at will.

The logic of indirect rule would now be extended throughout South Africa by the official appointment of local chiefs to preside over the reserves. In its public reports, the Native Affairs Department was careful to describe its role as that of recognizing existing chiefs, maintaining that only in "exceptional cases" was a chief appointed outside of the traditional process given by Native custom.[3] The department's own statistics, however, reveal an ever-expanding number of chiefs, from 384 in 1936, to 466 in 1945, and 701 in 1947.[4] Although state ethnologists, working from Isaac Schapera's *Bantu-Speaking Tribes of South Africa* and N. J. Van Warmelo's *Preliminary Survey of the Bantu Tribes of South Africa*,[5] began to compile lengthy genealogies of tribal and chiefly descent in an effort to keep careful track of the proper lines of hereditary authority, the department's correspondence files are filled with cases of deposed chiefs and disputed successions.[6]

The necessary complement to the state's assertion of control over the appointment and deposition of chiefs was its modification of the powers of chieftaincy. Chiefs were made officially responsible for carrying out all orders and instructions given to them by the local Native commissioner, as well as for the registration of taxpayers, the collection of taxes and population statistics, the allocation of land and prevention of illegal occupation and squatting, the detection and punishment of offenses, and the supply of labor when required.[7] The allocation of land may well have been within the scope of precolonial chieftaincy's authority, but "dispersing all riotous or unlawful assemblies of Natives" unquestionably was not.[8] Likewise, precolonial chiefly accumulation through the collection of tribute or the contribution of labor to the chief's fields corresponds at a surface level to the collection of taxes and the recruitment of labor, but its social context and material relevance are radically different. Precolonial chiefly accumulation operated as a form of social security for the community as a whole in times of crisis or for individual families in times of need.[9] The taxes levied on subsistence farming communities were meant to have the opposite effect, squeezing the resources available to rural households and forcing at least some members to leave in search of work in the cash economy.

Yet, extensive as these powers were, had the state simply wished to claim the right to make law for those categorized as Natives, the costuming of its administrative apparatus would have been entirely unnecessary. Brute supremacy could be had with nothing more than the *sjambok* and the machine gun. This, in effect, had been Botha's position in the segregation debate: white supremacy without apologies. The segregationists' argument was considerably more nuanced. By dressing the South African state in the costuming of tribal society and the institution of chieftaincy, its actions would become those of a separate social form, to which those classified as Natives could be said—with the full backing of modern anthropological science—to belong. What was being announced by the masking of the governor-general as the supreme chief was, thus, a claim to the right of representation. The state was not simply asserting the right to make law for black South Africans by proclamation, but to do so *as one of them*; to issue Native policy not from the mouth of a colonial administrator, but from that of an indigenous tribal chief.

The reason for this seemingly superfluous charade takes us to the heart of segregation's operation as a legitimation mechanism. The question of legitimacy concerns the conditions under which a subject grants obedience to an authority, without the need for coercive force to be employed or even threatened. The matter might be radically simplified if claims to authority within a particular social form were unique, exclusive, and monolithic. But the political environment is always and everywhere a competitive one, in which multiple voices call for the attention and loyalty of potential subjects. Where their demands conflict, how should I decide which to follow and which to ignore? The legitimation strategy of indirect rule answers by enfolding the question of authority's justification within that of its identity: the voice of authority to be obeyed is the one emanating from a figure with whom I share some common form of membership.

It is in this sense that Althusser's theory highlights the specular function of an ideological apparatus. In order to win my obedience, a potential authority must first succeed in convincing me that it is knocking on the correct door; that its commands really do concern me.[10] The ISA achieves this end by reflecting back to its subjects an image of themselves. Of course, were the ISA nothing more than a simple mirror, it might succeed in establishing a sense of identity, but fail to legitimate the relations of authority. The mirror, in this respect, contains a crucial flaw. The ordinary subject and the figure of authority (in Althusser's terms, the Absolute Subject) share a form of identity but are not perfectly identical to one another. If no distinctions could be drawn between them, why should one obey the other? The answer lies in Althusser's suggestion that the ideological apparatus is doubly speculary. The unlikeness of the reflection—the flaw in the image—is responsible for ordering the chain of command: "I am lesser than the Absolute Subject, therefore, I should obey him/her." But the power of the ISA comes from its ability to produce a sense of likeness as well: "I am similar to the Absolute Subject, therefore, I should follow him/her, instead of letting another voice win my allegiance." Thus, within the system of indirect rule, the position of chief was intended to produce both a sense of likeness—based upon images of racial and tribal identity—and a sense of hierarchical distinction. The first specular movement constructs a hierarchy; the second explains to concrete persons that its commands concern them in particular.

The Strains of Modernity

While tribal traditionalism lay at the center of the segregationist state's legitimation strategy, it existed side by side and in an unresolved oscillation with liberalism as an organizing concept and ideological frame for political identity in South Africa. During the colonial period, the line of demarcation between the two political strategies also marked a regional divide: traditionalist indirect rule in Natal and limited, modernist representative forms in the Cape. In the Transkei, under British rule, elected headmen rather than reconstituted tribal chiefs were placed in charge of rural communities.[11] Beginning in 1894, district councils were established to govern the annexed territories, and by 1930, the councils were amalgamated into the United Transkeian Territories General Council (UTTGC). The UTTGC itself was composed of twenty-six district magistrates, three councilors from each district, and three paramount chiefs holding *ex officio* membership. Not all districts recognized a paramount chief, however, and in some areas the institution of chieftaincy had disappeared entirely.[12] In one sense, the UTTGC was ultimately reined in by the power of the magistrates and the Native Affairs Department to nominate representatives. Yet, in other ways the council could be seen as a mechanism informed by and working towards a type of political liberalism. As industrialization pulled ever-increasing numbers of black workers to the cities and extended the range of contact between blacks and whites in the rural areas, the UTTGC was frequently referred to as a means through which Africans would receive training in the operation of "modern constitutional government."[13] In at least one case, this is precisely what occurred. In 1946, the council broke ranks with its government patrons, issuing a call for the extension of a direct individual franchise to all black South Africans.[14]

The liberal tendency recognizable in the UTTGC was replicated at the national level in 1936 by the Representation of Natives Act.[15] According to the act, each of four regional districts (Natal, the Transvaal and the Orange Free State, the Transkei, and the Cape) would elect one member of the country's forty-eight seat Senate through voting units composed of the existing local-level representatives: local councils, regional authorities, Native advisory boards, or where these did not exist, chiefs and headmen. The exist-ing race-neutral voters' roll in the Cape was bifurcated, and the Cape divided into three electoral units from which black voters already on the rolls would elect one member each to the House of Assembly as Natives representatives. Finally, the act created a Natives Representatives Council (NRC) composed of the secretary for Native affairs, five nominated chief Native commission-ers, four members nominated by the governor-general, and twelve members elected by the regional voting units.

The form of representation offered by the act was patently undemocratic and, as Marian Lacey has argued, bent in the direction of traditionalism by enshrining chiefs as the dominant force in rural electoral colleges.[16] But the creation of the NRC (frequently referred to by politicians and journalists as "the black parliament") also carried with it the same liberalizing, assimila-tionist impulses contained within the UTTGC. Where indirect rule and seg-regation suggested an eternal inevitability to the institution of chieftaincy, the NRC appeared as an apparatus through which tribal chiefs would even-tually be supplanted by modern representative bodies. And though limited in its capacity for governance, it seems briefly to have served as a staging area for resistance to segregation. An analysis of the elections held under the Natives Representatives Act revealed the success after 1939 of increasingly militant candidates calling for racial equality.[17] Within a few years, however, the limits of the NRC as a venue for antisegregationist politics became clear. In 1946, following the government's continued rejection of their recom-mendations, the elected members of the NRC voted to adjourn in protest.

The tension between traditionalist and liberal modes of interpellation also surfaced at the Native Commissioners' Conference in November 1945. The positions expressed there are worth quoting at some length, as they offer an unusual insight into the Native Affairs Department's perception of an impending modernization crisis and its potential solution. A debate over the issue of chieftaincy was sparked when the Native Commissioner for Ndwedwe moved that the system of indirect rule had become "inefficient and unprogressive" and should be gradually replaced by a system substitut-ing elected representatives for hereditary chiefs:

> Native Commissioner, Ndwedwe: I feel that the justification of this motion is to hear what the Department's views are, and what the Government's policy is going to be. . . . I would like to emphasize the fact that with the advances made in edu-cation, there are a tremendous number of educated Natives and one of the diffi-culties with the chiefs is that they are illiterate. They are not competent to administer justice. They have some idea of the principles necessary in dealing with matters that are purely customary, but the time is approaching when the system is going to be unsatisfactory. . . . There are about 28 chiefs in my district, who all regard themselves as Chiefs [*sic*]. One or two are quite good, but all are illiterate, keep no records, cases reported are frequently quite wrong, they do not carry out

duties themselves but send indunas and tribal constables. The present system is not very satisfactory. I do not know how it is going to be improved if we rely on hereditary right. We have no method by which the election of suitable men can be brought about. I submit the motion more for guidance than anything else.

Native Commissioner, Nongoma: I do not know whether Mr. Liefeldt has read the "Ilanga lase Natal," the Natives' paper for Natal. There you will see definite attack by the educated native on the tribal system. They want to do away entirely with these posts of Chiefs. The time is not quite ripe yet to do away with our Chiefs. No one will argue that they are efficient, but at the same time I do not feel that they are entirely to blame. . . . The weakness of the whole system of tribal organization lies in the fact that the Chief is not put through a course of training to fit him for his job. . . . His training must have an agricultural bias, as our rehabilitation organization will call for men with sufficient agricultural knowledge. He must also be taught something about judicial work. He does not know the first thing about trying cases or Native custom. I am right in saying that the greatest trouble we have is to unravel cases tried by Native Chiefs. That is largely due to the fact that the Chief does not know what his job is. . . . The Chiefs must also be employed at reasonable rates of pay. We cannot expect efficiency from a Chief who is paid 10/- per month. My kitchen boy gets £4 per month. I suggest that the time has arrived when we should rebuild our tribes as they existed in the olden days.

Native Commissioner, Harding: We are agreed that we cannot do without our Native Chiefs. If we take away the Chiefs, we destroy the last link holding the Natives together and we lay the way open to Communism or any other reform. We have taken away so much of the Chiefs' power that they are developing into "yes" men. They have the privileges of Chiefs but no responsibility. . . . We have to back up the Chiefs as much as possible, but one obstacle is in regard to agitators. In former days when a Chief had an agitator, he was got rid of and the Chief maintained his prestige. Today the agitator preaches whatever he likes, but it is difficult to get such a Native removed and the Chiefs are losing heart.[18]

Though, in this case, the lines were drawn between traditionalist and liberal impulses (rather than between traditionalism and an unalloyed white supremacism), the contours of the debate over the future of chieftaincy run precisely parallel to those of the segregation debate four decades earlier: a desire to find some correspondence between objective social conditions and the form of political representation was posed against a desire to use the latter to paper-over the unwanted contradictions of the former.

Opinion at the Native Commissioners' Conference leaned against the Commissioner for Ndwedwe's suggestions, and the debate concluded with a decision to produce and distribute a handbook for chiefs. But liberal alternatives to the grander edifices of segregation had their backers elsewhere in the state. The 1946–48 Fagan Commission, convened to reexamine the Native Question, reported in its findings that Africans and Europeans had become thoroughly "economically intertwined" and, therefore, should be accepted as being "parts of the same big machine."[19] The task of the state in this situation was to "ease friction" in the machine, giving up on the pursuit of segregation where it was unworkable, but defending it where integrated institutions might lead to conflict.[20] Set against the liberal notion of a capitulation to market forces (limited only by the palatability of racial integration), traditionalism, paradoxically, offered the more daring vision of social engineering: chiefs were to be instructed in Native custom, tribes were to be rebuilt, and modernity forcibly turned back.

A more impressionistic picture of these contradictory impulses can be drawn from the South African state's own propaganda. In 1947, the State Information Office produced a pamphlet intended to defend Native policy in the union against the growing wave of postwar anticolonial sentiment.[21] Its central claim was for the policy of "trusteeship," arguing that South Africa had done far more than other African nations in bringing the benefits of economic progress to the Natives. Perhaps more revealing than its text— detailing South African progress in agriculture, education, and heath care— are the photographs chosen for inclusion alongside. Perfectly reflecting the state's own oscillating paradigms of interpellation, they depict, on alternate pages, the tribal Native and the detribalized urbanite: a woman wrapped in a blanket, "Queen Modjaje . . . [who] wields as much power as the bringer of rain as did her predecessors in the last century," next to the members of the Natives Representatives Council in suits and ties; village huts in Bavendaland and township houses in Stellenbosch; "Native cinema goers" above "traditional Native war dancers." The war dances, readers were assured, "are seldom performed to-day in the reserves, but they are encouraged in the compounds of the Witwatersrand gold mines."[22]

Apartheid and Separate Development

The apartheid policies developed during the 1950s and 1960s by the NP government do not have any precise origin as a single, cohesive political agenda.[23] But one of the central features of the restructuring of segregation was an effort to end the unstable oscillation between liberalism and traditionalism with regard to black South Africans by fusing both tendencies into the new paradigm of *separate development.* Traditionalist ideological apparatuses would be enhanced and revitalized, but certain of the promises of liberalism would also be offered up: equal rights, representative government, and economic development—the proviso being that these would be granted only within racially, tribally, or ethnically exclusive areas.[24]

The desire to reinforce the ideology of tribal tradition during the early 1950s is especially visible in the Native Affairs Department's annual reports for those years, and their contrast with the reports produced under the United Party government of the late 1940s is particularly striking. The final pages of the NAD report for 1945–47 featured a fold-out photograph depicting the visit of the British royalty to a Johannesburg township. The caption reads: "At Orlando, in Johannesburg, the biggest Native township in the Union, it is estimated that upwards of 100,000 Africans of all tribes lined the streets as Their Majesties drove to the Community Hall."[25] The crowd in the photo is unremarkable for an urban setting circa 1946, dressed in contemporary European suits, coats, and hats. In 1951–52, the department chose to portray the population under its administration rather differently. In that year's report, black South Africans were represented by "A Xhosa woman enjoying her pipe" and "A young Pondo Girl," both dressed in blankets and beads.[26] Corresponding with the frequently repeated dictum that blacks were only to be present in the urban areas as "temporary workers," official depictions of the black population shifted from city streets to village huts, from modernity to tradition.[27]

Government officials also began a concerted effort to weed out potential inconsistencies and contradictions in their references to race. The historical and political implications of the term "Native" had been pointed out in 1932 by the Native Economic Commission, which noted in its report: "It is not a very suitable word, however, inasmuch as it excludes all other people who are likewise 'native' to the country, it also leads to such contradictions as 'indigenous natives' and 'foreign natives.' "[28] Though potentially derogatory in its suggestion of colonial notions of primitivism, "Native" also carried with it the distinct implication of belonging. A native has been there all along. It is only the foreigner—the colonist, the settler—who is able to point and stare at the natives. The 1932 Commission employed the term "Abantu" in its report (redeploying the name of a linguistic group as a marker of race), but its usage failed to catch on in other state organs. By the early 1950s, some in government circles were once again pressing for the substitution of "Bantu" for "Native." In 1958, under Hendrik Verwoerd's administration, the shift became official policy.[29]

Similarly, the 1950s saw a renewed focus on the concept of tribal identity. The 1946 photo of Orlando whose caption described it as depicting thousands of "Africans of all tribes," admitted, in effect, to the urban integration of linguistic groups the ethnological section of the Native Affairs Department had once worked so diligently to distinguish analytically. To reveal that Xhosas, Pondos, Zulus, and Sothos all lived next door to one another in the townships and came out together to wave to the queen was dangerously close to an admission that in urban areas, the notion of tribe had little relevance. After 1950, the slippage was reversed. The captioning of the 1951 and 52 photos positions the tribal designation as the most significant identifier of each woman. They are each shown standing alone—solitary, emblematic representatives of their tribal groups. Any white South African schoolchild who consulted his or her *Race Studies* text would know immediately what sort of hut each woman lived in, what sort of pottery she spent her days making, and what traditional foods she ate.[30] In 1936, the minister for Native Affairs bemoaned the proliferation of, "a new class of detribalized Native who has . . . lost the conservatism and restraints of the old life," while in 1950, the chief Native commissioner for Natal reported that during the previous year, "tribal life continued much as it always has done."[31]

The dilemma, of course, for the leaders of the nascent apartheid state was that the very elements revealing the nonexistence of a separate tribal social formation—migrant labor and the increasingly permanent presence of a black working class in the urban areas—were objectively necessary conditions of South African society as they knew it and wished it to be. Tribal life could not possibly continue as it always had done, but perhaps it could be restored and reinvigorated as an ideological apparatus. To this end, the 1951 Bantu Authorities Act provided for the uniform establishment of tribal authorities, consisting of a chief or headman and a tribal council appointed by the chief, although the Native commissioner retained the right to veto any appointment and to directly appoint members to the council.[32] Tribal authorities were empowered to administer the affairs of a tribe, to assist the government in its administration of the area, and to maintain a treasury into which judicial fines collected by the chief or fees taken in accordance with "recognized customs" were paid. As a replacement for the NRC, the Bantu Authorities Act would, in the words of the minister for Native Affairs, provide for the "restoration of the prestige, the authority of Native law and custom."[33]

The replacement of the NRC with local-level chieftaincies marked a decisive shift away from the notion of political representation through popular election. As the undersecretary for Native Affairs put the case, chieftaincy was an hereditary institution:

> The chiefs and headmen are leaders by virtue of their birthright and traditional tribal law. If then they are leaders by birthright or by tribal law, then there is no need to elect them to a position which they already hold.[34]

The 1951 act, though, defined chiefs as persons appointed or recognized as such under the provisions of the 1927 Native Administration Act, suggesting a somewhat different mechanism for chiefly succession. By the Native Affairs Department's own admission, following the introduction of Bantu Authorities, "a considerable number of new tribal chiefs were appointed."[35] The reasons for maintaining final authority over the appointment of chiefs were clear: the apartheid state could not risk the possibility of one of its local-level functionaries becoming a resistance leader, without retaining the power to remove such a person from office immediately. But the continued fixation on the myth of hereditary succession served to underscore the ideological functions of the Bantu Authorities Act. A chief whose mandate of authority depended entirely upon the state was nothing more than an appointed rural administrator. As the earlier generation of indirect rule seg-regationists had realized, a hereditary chief might appear to be something more. Hereditary authority was arguably incontestable, not subject to popu-lar election or review. More importantly, its apparent source was not the state, but a tradition internal to the tribal society over which it held sway.

Thus, in appointing chiefs to the new tribal authorities, government offi-cials were particularly concerned to locate someone not only willing to col-laborate with apartheid, but behind whom a chiefly lineage could be "discovered" by the anthropologists and ethnologists specially called in for the task.[36] The creation of tribal councils, the Bantu Authorities Act's primary innovation, reflected the same schizophrenic combination of a meticulous attention to the details of precolonial African social organization and their total disregard. As David Hammond-Tooke pointed out, the state recognized in the act the fact that precolonial chiefs had exercised their powers through and in consultation with a council.[37] Precolonial chiefs' councils, though, were not nominated bodies but groups of a community's adult men, varying in size and membership. A chief could make no important decision without consulting a general meeting of all adult men.[38] By 1951, most of a rural com-munity's adult men would have been working or seeking work in the cities, in the mines, or on the large commercial farms, and the reconstructed tribal councils could only have been bodies whose membership was filled out by functionaries not only nominated but paid by the state.

While in this sense the Bantu Authorities Act was intended to produce a form of ideological costuming directly traceable to the strategies of indirect rule, it was in another respect an unmasking and a transference of the imagery. The 1927 Native Administration Act's masking of the governor-general as supreme chief left him still entirely recognizable as an arm of the state. With the Bantu Authorities Act, the state would remove the mask and place it instead on the chiefs themselves, sharpening the distinction between white South Africa and the black tribal society. The government's own belief in the power of its new ideological machinery is reflected in a memorandum sent from the secretary of the Native Affairs Department (soon to be renamed as the Department of Bantu Administration and Development) to the local commissioner in Pietermaritzburg, instructing him that the design and construction of facilities for tribal authorities should conform, "as far as possible, with Bantu culture and tradition."[39] The comments of one field administrator in a correspondence with the commissioner's office, however, make clear the more material purposes of the act:

> I shall be glad if the Bantu Affairs Commissioner will submit concrete proposals for the establishment of a tribal authority for Chief Sekgopa's tribe. At the same time the conferment of civil and criminal jurisdiction on the Chief will be consid-ered. Once these steps have been taken, the Chief and his Council can proceed

against agitators according to the tribal laws and traditions and if such action fails, consideration will be given to proceeding against the agitators in terms of section 5 of Act 38 of 1927.[40]

For all of its traditionalist costuming and supporting rhetoric declaring the resurrection of traditional tribal government, the Bantu Authorities Act also betrayed a renewed desire to appeal to the mores of Western representative democracy. And while racial segregation in South Africa was increasingly coming under international scrutiny in the 1950s and 1960s, the apartheid state's efforts to speak in the language of democracy was by no means aimed at foreign audiences exclusively. It was also during this period that the African National Congress (ANC) became a leading force in organizing the black working class to resist segregation, consolidating its political position in favor of nonracial democracy—a stand informed and strengthened by the anticolonial movements taking shape in the rest of the continent. Responding to both foreign and domestic calls for democracy, governing NP leaders defended their new policy with a quasi-Hegelian vision of national self-expression:

> Here we have a basis on which the Native will henceforth be able to give expression to his own inner self, to develop his family life and his national life. Henceforth, according to this Bill, he will have the opportunity also to be a recipient of those human rights and privileges for which we are all yearning in this life.[41]

Attempting to maneuver its way through the glaring contradiction between representative democracy and hereditary rule, the Department of Bantu Administration and Development now described chieftaincy as "the traditional Bantu democracy . . . [providing] shelter under which the highest and the lowest can feel at home and find self-expression and fulfillment."[42]

Appropriate to this new spirit of democracy, the establishment of a tribal authority was said to be voluntary and to result from a process of consultation.[43] The actual process was something of a traveling road show in which Bantu Administration officials met with groups of chiefs, gave speeches on the new system, and fielded questions from the crowd. The degree to which anyone present believed in the voluntary nature of the proceedings, though, is put into doubt by some of the existing transcripts. A meeting in 1955 with several chiefs in Natal, including Zulu king Cyprian Bekhuzulu, for example, produced the following exchange:

> Chief Cyprian: As it is law it is difficult to comment on it. If it had not been, I would have one question: have we not been doing the right thing all along?

> Native Commissioner: I do not say that you have not been doing the right thing, the Government wants to give it a legal form.

Chief Pumanyova: We have not yet been in a settled position about the Bantu Educational Act and today we are faced with the Bantu Authorities Act. It appears to me that the Government had been working on these Acts long before my father was born, and it is only now put into operation. How can I who do not know the advantages and disadvantages of this be expected to accept this Act?

Native Commissioner: I presume you have a council which you consult in tribal matters. The Bantu Authority is the same except that it will be constituted according to the Act.

Chief Moses: What I want to know is why did the government not force this on us instead of obtaining our views? It is difficult for any human being to be given a stick to thrash himself, some one else must do the thrashing.

Native Commissioner: What must I report to the Department?

Chief Cyprian: We are not against the Government, we do not say we are against the Act. It is however our desire that what we have said here today should be forwarded to the authorities. I say this because it is the first occasion we have had to discuss this Act fully. We received the pamphlets, and we have never dealt so fully with the matter as we have done today.[44]

But it was also in Natal that a degree of resistance was encountered from chiefs expressing concern that the institutionalization of a tribal council would amount to a reduction of their powers.[45] The historical irony here was that the chiefs had become comfortably accustomed to the Shepstonian version of traditional authority: the investment of local power in the hands of the chief as a lone individual. What state officials held up as a restoration of traditional tribal institutions, several chiefs interpreted as an attack on them. As Cyprian stated in a letter to the Native commissioner for Nongoma,

I cannot hide the fact that there is danger in this Bantu Authorities Act, as we shall now be controlled by the Council, it means, that our status has been lowered. It is obvious to me that this Act has brought about the fall of our Zulu power.[46]

There was also the matter of money. Under the act fines and fees previously paid to the chief himself would now be paid into a fund controlled by the tribal authority as a body. This, too, might have raised the potential for resistance, as chiefs saw their sources of income and patronage disappear, had the new policy not included a revised system for the payment of chiefs. Under the 1927 act, chiefs could expect to receive irregular allowances from the state, but were only paid yearly salaries if in addition to being recognized as chiefs they were also designated as local headmen.[47] The Bantu Authorities Act promised to bring all chiefs, as the heads of tribal authorities, onto the payroll and to significantly increase their salaries. Previously, headmen had received a starting salary of £12 per annum, rising to £32 after sixteen years good service. By the mid-1950s this was raised to a scale from £60 to £144, with paramount chiefs in the Transkei receiving from £600 to £1200.[48]

Both the salary increases for chiefs and the administrative reorganization of rural local governments were tied to the larger process of agricultural transformation.[49] The racial segregation of landholding after 1913 and the severe limitation on the amount of land available to blacks were originally intended as mechanisms to insure the availability of wage labor. By the 1930s, however, the device had worked all too well, resulting in the severe impoverishment of the Transkei.[50] Various proposals for stock-culling were floated during the 1930s and by the late 1940s, the government began attempts to carry out betterment programs involving stock-culling, fencing, and land rehabilitation. The simultaneous imposition of stricter controls on the movement of black workers into the cities, however, meant that rural families were caught in a vicious double bind. Land rehabilitation promised better agricultural conditions, but only for fewer people raising fewer cattle and smaller crops. The urban areas offered opportunities for those who might now be squeezed off of the land, but the reinvigorated program of racial segregation and labor control stood in their way. For those who remained in the rural areas, the betterment schemes became a source of deep resentment. Stock-culling was particularly feared by rural families, for whom cattle represented the primary form of household capital. The work of hoeing weeds and digging firebreaks was often carried out using forced labor, amounting to even greater losses of income for peasants trapped in the land rehabilitation process.[51]

As resistance to the rehabilitation programs arose, Bantu Administration officials worked to insure that the chiefs remained a barrier between themselves and angry rural villagers. One case occurred during July 1959, in Natal, when a group of about 450 women who had worked for four years on the construction of a firebreak (without pay and using their own tools) began a series of protests and deputations to the office of the local Bantu Affairs commissioner.[52] On each of several occasions, the women were asked by the commissioner to indicate which tribe they belonged to and who their chief was. They were then informed that the government could only hear their complaints through representation of the tribal authority. Shortly afterward, the chief of Northern Natal's only functioning tribal authority received an anonymous letter:

> You will regret your attitude of accepting the Bantu Authorities because all your kraal [household] and inmates will die. If you think you want to be in the European's good books by accepting Bantu Authorities, you are wrong, you are merely displaying to them your foolishness. . . . You should know that the people are fully prepared to die, and you will also die with them. . . . Our hearts are really sore for our country.[53]

By 1961, the Bantu Administration Department had established *ad hoc* militias ("homeguards") for chiefs and councilors in Bantu Authorities areas.[54]

In several instances during the 1950s and early 1960s, local organizing to resist the betterment schemes developed into militant—though short-lived—resistance to the state. In the Tsolo district of the Transkei, an anti-stock-theft organization, the *Makhuluspani* [Big Team], gradually transformed into a political movement, carrying out actions against chiefs and headmen who were seen to be collaborating with the government in the establishment of Bantu Authorities.[55] In the Mt. Ayliff district, the politics of indirect rule chieftaincy collided with both socialism and racial nationalism. In 1946, a stock-culling program was initiated in the district with the collaboration of Gaulibaso Kaiser Jojo, state-appointed chief for the Xesibe community.[56] Within a year, popular opposition to the program began to be expressed at public meetings, which increasingly gravitated around the figure of Ntlabati Jojo, Gaulibaso's younger brother, who since 1938 had maintained a claim to the chieftaincy. In October 1949, a group of nearly 200 Xesibe residents visited the office of the district commissioner, where the following exchange took place:

> Bambata Mageleti of Sidakeni Location: We Xesibes have a complaint. We ask you to meet us in the District in Dundee location. We do not want the present Chief.

> Tiki Nkosana of Dundee Location: I second the first speaker. In the place of the present Chief we appoint Ntlabati Kwalukwalu.

> Bambata Mageleti: We ask you as the Government Representative of the District to go out and listen to what we have to say. We have already appointed Ntlabati as our Chief. According to custom the people nominate a Chief and the appointment is confirmed by the Government Representative.

> Native Commissioner: But you have a Chief.

> Bambata Mageleti: Gaulibaso does not associate with us. We do not know the reason for his attitude.[57]

When their request was refused, Ntlabati's supporters retained a lawyer in Port Elizabeth to plead his case. On the surface, the resistance to stock-culling in Mt. Ayliff would appear to have been fully invested in the institution of chieftaincy, concerned only to replace a "bad" chief with a "good" one. But behind the scenes, the opposition had formed itself into an organization called the Kongo, taken up arms, and affiliated with the All African Convention (a Trotskyite resistance group), perhaps as early as 1948.[58] Ntlabati himself appears to have been a member of the Kongo, but later renounced his membership and his claim to the chieftaincy in an unsuccessful bid to avoid being exiled to a distant province in Natal.[59]

Quoting E. P. Thompson, Colin Bundy describes rural resistance movements like the one in Mt. Ayliff as "rebellious, but rebellious in defense of custom."[60] Such a description fails, however, to describe adequately the range of response to Bantu Authorities and the agricultural betterment schemes. In some instances, collaborating chiefs were attacked and killed by their subjects.[61] In other cases, chiefs became involved in leading opposition to the state, were deposed by government officials, and were deported to distant parts of the country.[62] During the women's protest in Natal, when asked by the local commissioner who their chief was, many of the women responded that they had none and insisted that their protest be received directly rather than through any form of representation.[63] The Mt. Ayliff conflict suggests a particularly complex interplay in which the authority of chieftaincy was simultaneously acknowledged and transcended. In this case, custom was not so much defended as it was utilized in pursuit of broader political goals of a distinctly modern character. If indirect rule proposed to cloak the segregationist state's agenda in the trappings of precolonial tradition, the Kongo threatened to turn the tables, dressing its own version of modernity—Trotskyite African nationalism—in chiefly robes.[64]

A similar maneuver had been attempted in 1928 by a council of chiefs organized under the aegis of the ANC to protest passage of the Native Administration Act. In a pamphlet entitled *The Powers of the Supreme Chief,* the chiefs' council made the case that the institutions of indirect rule chieftaincy bore no resemblance to those of precolonial times.[65] Chieftaincy, the council argued, was a hereditary office, over which no higher authority held powers of appointment or deposition. No chief could take action on a matter concerning his community without first consulting his uncles and brothers and ultimately receiving the approval of the *pitso,* an assembly that "every male person of age is expected to attend."[66] Autocratic powers of rule by proclamation, they maintained, were unheard of. Woven into their critique of indirect rule, however, was a tangible flirtation with the notion of racial difference as a basis for political representation:

> The African National Congress, of which this Council of Chiefs is an integral part, is strongly opposed to the policy of segregation unless by it is meant the creation of two States, one European and the other Native. We cannot see how two peoples, living in the same country and under the same governmental control, can develop separate nationalities and separate civilizations. It is our firm conviction that the Bantu people can develop along their own lines if they have a country of their own and are free from European interference. However, if it is the policy of the Government that the Bantu people should be governed by means of their own laws and customs, we feel it our duty, as guardians of the people, to point out that this should be in accordance with native law and not with the wishes of the white race.[67]

The chiefs' council's alternative to a segregated South Africa was not quite the modernist vision of nonracial liberalism or socialism held in other quarters of the ANC, but a conservative, traditionalist separatism.

Such conservatism in black politics, however, would soon fall out of fashion. The chiefs' council within the ANC was dissolved in 1943, and by the

1950s, the broadest forces of mass resistance to segregation were set in distinctly modernist frames. Anton Lembede, the principle founder of African nationalism in South Africa, wrote of the new philosophy:

> The African natives then live and move and have their being in the spirit of Africa; in short they are one with Africa. It is then this spirit of Africa which is the common factor of cooperation and the basis of unity among African tribes; it is African Nationalism or Africanism. So that all Africans must be converted from tribalism into African Nationalism, which is a higher step or degree of the self-expression and self-realization of the African spirit, Africa through her spirit is using us to develop that higher quality of Africanism. We have then to go out as apostles to preach the new gospel of Africanism and to hasten and bring about the birth of a new nation. Such minor insignificant differences of languages, customs, etc. will not hinder or stop the irresistible onward surge of the African spirit.[68]

African nationalist rhetoric occasionally carried with it an echo of traditionalism, at times invoking the names of chiefs who had resisted colonial occupation and rule.[69] But the call to transcend tribal identities and forge a new nation clearly looked beyond any imagined resurrection of precolonial society. African nationalism in the 1950s conceived of itself as a movement to bring black South Africans into the modern world against the wishes of a state that sought to hold them forever in the past.

Where the nationalist movement of the 1950s eventually divided was over the importance and meaning of the race paradigm. The segregationist strategy of the 1920s had been founded on a notion of race whose primary imperative was the differentiation of Europeans from Africans. Yet, within this form of racialization lay an implicit suggestion of the political unity of the group it aimed to oppress. As a leader of the ANC Youth League in its early years, Lembede rooted his vision of African nationalism in precisely this contradiction. The anticolonialism expressed by the early Youth League and by the inheritor of its political tradition, the Pan-Africanist Congress (PAC), conceived of whites as foreign settlers and blacks as the indigenous, rightful rulers of the African continent.[70] Anticolonialism, in this version, meant an acceptance of the political validity of race. The racially segregated society, however, contained deeper contradictions, from which a very different politics might emerge. Daily life in segregated South Africa was experienced as the constant interaction and interdependence of individuals who were socially identified and politically represented as members of separate racial groups. The creation of an alliance between the ANC and antiapartheid organizations representing whites, coloreds, and Indians was intended to overcome this contradiction. The Freedom Charter, adopted in 1955 as the Congress Alliance's statement of principle, declared South Africa to belong to all who lived in it, pointing past even multiracialism to the political irrelevance of racial identity.

The broad resistance to apartheid thus spoke simultaneously to a racialized anticolonialism and a deracialized national democratic sentiment. In the work of the 1950–54 Tomlinson Commission, we can recognize the state's attempt to respond on both fronts. Its mission was "to conduct an exhaustive inquiry into and to report upon a comprehensive scheme for the rehabilitation of the Native areas with a view to developing within them a social structure in keeping with the culture of the Native and based on effective socio-economic planning."[71] Reversing the conclusions of the Fagan Commission, the Tomlinson report was intended to lay scientific foundations for a vast new system of segregation. While the Bantu Authorities Act had aimed at a reinforcement of the race paradigm by effecting a white withdrawal from the political representation of blacks, it left unsolved the problems of a white minority faced with the growing political demands of a black majority left unrepresented in the modern state. How could apartheid's racial hierarchy be upheld while simultaneously answering the demands for an end to white colonial rule? The Tomlinson Commission's squaring of this circle began by reconceptualizing the building blocks of social and political identity, subdividing the concept of race into a collection of ethnicities—at least for blacks. Among its other findings, the commission reported that

> the European population . . . has developed into an autonomous and complete national organism, and has furthermore preserved its character as a biological entity. There are not the slightest grounds for believing that the European population . . . would be willing to sacrifice its character as a national entity and as a European racial group, [whereas] the Bantu peoples . . . do not constitute a homogeneous people, but form separate national units on the basis of language and culture.[72]

Rather than the Fagan Commission's "one big machine," South African society was now conceived of as a "nation of minorities," each deserving of its own territorial homeland and separate system of political representation.[73]

The 1959 Promotion of Bantu Self-Government Act defined eight such national units—North Sotho, South Sotho, Tswana, Zulu, Swazi, Xhosa, Tsonga, and Venda—to which persons formerly race-classified as Native or Bantu would now be linked.[74] Subsequent legislation in the early 1970s provided for the transformation of the ethnic home regions from self-governing territories into politically independent nation-states. Describing separate development's guiding principles, minister of Native Affairs M. D. C. De Wet Nel seemed to speak directly to Anton Lembede's plea for the African spirit to be freed from colonial rule:

> The first is that God has given a divine task and calling to every People in the world, which dare not be destroyed or denied by anyone. The second is that every

People in the world of whatever race or colour, just like every individual, has the inherent right to live and develop. Every People is entitled to the right of self-preservation. In the third place it is our deep conviction that the personal and national ideals of every ethnic group can best be developed within its own national community.[75]

But along with its reinterpretation of race and ethnicity, the new policy also included a radically revised regional history, according to which migrating groups of Africans and Europeans had arrived simultaneously in the territories that now comprised South Africa. The areas demarcated as ethnic homelands were declared to be the same as those previously occupied by African tribes. Not an inch of ground had changed hands due to colonialism.[76]

The first prototype was to be the Transkei. In 1963, the territory was given its own legislative assembly, cabinet, chief minister, flag, and national anthem.[77] In the structure of its political institutions, the homelands or Bantustan system reflected the same unstable mixture of traditionalism and liberalism found in the Bantu Authorities Act, combining the notion of hereditary authority with the concept of democratic representation. Bantustan citizenship thus included the right to elect representatives to the homeland's legislative assembly, although the majority of seats were automatically assigned to appointed chiefs. The bizarre nature of the experiment inspired a flurry of scholarship devoted primarily to analyses of the economic and political viability of the homelands.[78] Geographically, the Bantustans were the same rural reserves set aside for African land ownership by the 1913 and 1936 Land Acts, amounting to no more than thirteen percent of the country and severely lacking in economic resources and infrastructure. Further, the national units into which the reserves were amalgamated remained territorially fragmented due to the government's imperative to avoid dispossessing white landowners of their property. The reserves had originally been designed as sources of migrant labor. As most analysts pointed out, Bantustan independence was never seriously intended to alter the flow of workers to the mines and commercial farms. In the words of a government circular explaining the policy:

It is accepted Government policy that the Bantu are only temporarily resident in the European areas of the Republic, for as long as they offer their labour there. As soon as they become, for one reason or another, no longer fit for work or superfluous in the labour market, they are expected to return to their country of origin, or the territory of the national unit where they fit in ethnically if they were not born and bred in the homeland. . . . [N]o stone is to be left unturned to achieve the settlement in the homelands of non-productive Bantu at present residing in the European areas.[79]

As Butler, Rotberg, and Adams noted in their study of Bophuthatswana and KwaZulu, more than three quarters of each homeland's national income

came from absentee labor.[80] In the Transkei, widely considered to be separate development's best chance for success, there were in 1976 no more
than 50,000 paying jobs to accommodate a resident population of over
1.6 million.[81] As with the earlier versions of segregation in South Africa, the
claim that racialized groups constituted separate social forms was denied by
their organic connection through the migrant labor system. As Roger
Southall argued in his assessment of Transkeian "independence," the
Bantustans could only be understood as integral components of the wider
South African political economy.[82]

As an ideological strategy, separate development was not so much a new
innovation as a retooling of the old segregationist machinery. The construction of parliament buildings and the raising of national flags over the former
reserves were meant to renew and to reinforce their long-standing purpose
as costumes for the state. But the specific intent behind the Bantustan
scheme was to usher the strategy of indirect rule into the contemporary
political environment by teaching it the language of anticolonialism and
national self-determination. The quasi-Hegelian rhetoric with which NP
politicians proclaimed the beauty and humanity of the homelands policy
was, in this sense, deeply suggestive of separate development's political
agenda. For as much as Hegel saw in liberal citizenship a means with which
to calm the waters stirred by capitalism—membership in the state healing
the divisions of civil society—the NP saw in Bantustan citizenship a way to
quiet the storm rising against racial segregation. If modernity had somehow
flown out of control, sending ever more black workers into the cities, threatening to make the tribal institutions of indirect rule obsolete, separate development proposed to offer just enough liberal nationalism to make
segregation viable once again. If the tribe, the chief, and the rustic hut were
not enough, perhaps the nation, the chief minister, and the legislative assembly would be.

Of course, high-speed ethnonationalization was not without its ambiguities and contradictions. In the early 1960s, the UTTGC offered the unique
possibility of an already-existing political apparatus that could be pressed
into service as a regional homeland government. But the rapid transformation of the Transkei into South Africa's first Bantustan left behind a considerable number of Xhosa-speaking communities in the adjacent Ciskei. The
eventual development of the Ciskei as its own self-governing territory meant
that there would now be two Xhosa-speaking homelands with no apparent
ethnic, linguistic, or cultural distinction between them.[83] As one study of a
village in the "independent" Transkei noted, the purported ethnic nations
remained ethnolinguistically diverse. Out of 162 households in the village of
St. Paul's, the vast majority (116) were Sotho-speakers, but the population
also included Xhosas, Hlubis, and a number of "mixed marriages."[84] Despite
the forced removal and relocation of over 3.5 million people between 1960

and 1983, the national spirits of the officially assigned ethnic groups stubbornly refused to develop and express themselves separately.

The impetus behind separate development's grand design was clear. Political opposition to white supremacist rule was on the rise and—in the eyes of South Africa's segregationist leaders—was directly connected to the urbanization and detribalization of the black working class:

> In the past year, in several parts of the country, malicious opposition was experienced, apparently organised from our large cities through means of partly detribalized Natives.[85]

> [S]trong influences have been at work in the effort to destroy everything connected with the national character of the Natives. That steady background of his tribal consciousness and of his tribal links is gradually disappearing, and the Native is . . . suspended in mid-air; he has a feeling of instability which is nourished by people who are only too eager that he should be torn away from his anchors, so that he can become easy prey to their propaganda.[86]

Yet, the material realities of the country's increasingly industrialized economy meant that the apartheid dream of a South Africa in which only whites would reside permanently in the urban areas would always remain a fantasy. Thus, not long after passage of the Promotion of Bantu Self-Government Act, an additional piece of legislation was introduced, aimed at bringing the principles of indirect rule to the segregated urban townships.

The 1961 Urban Bantu Councils Act provided for the establishment of governing councils within black residential areas in the cities. The councils' powers were unspecified by the act, left open to be defined by government and subject to revocation at any time.[87] Much like the other components of separate development, the new law appeared to fuse traditionalist and modernist elements within the basic framework of indirect rule. The councils' membership would be made up of both elected and appointed representatives, with the appointed members being nominated by chiefs' representatives in each urban district. According to the Department of Bantu Administration and Development,

> [t]he idea of chiefs being represented in urban areas originated spontaneously among the Bantu and by the Urban Bantu Councils Act . . . the government gave recognition to the scheme. The purpose of the scheme is to preserve contact with the urban Bantu and, in so doing, to prevent tribal disruption, estrangement and other problems.[88]

The department apparently had every hope that, "the Bantu who in the course of time have become estranged [would] gradually return to the fold," but the reception given to the chiefs' urban representatives was often somewhat less than welcoming.[89] Reporting on a 1961 visit by a chief to Cape Town's segregated urban districts, sociologist Archie Mafeje found that "Westernized Africans" dismissed chieftaincy as an outdated and irrelevant institution; while even recent migrants from the rural areas felt that it had been perverted by its association with the apartheid state.[90] Transkeian chief Kaiser Matanzima reported the same findings after visiting Johannesburg's Soweto townships in the mid-1960s.[91]

More modest attempts at the retribalization of black workers on commercial farms and mine sites met with similar results. On the one hand, the establishment of labor bureaus within tribal areas defined by the Bantu Authorities Act created the possibility for at least partial canalization of migrant labor along ethnolinguistic lines, and workers' housing on some mine sites was segregated by ethnicity.[92] On the other hand, though, the conditions of work on the farms and in the mines necessarily brought migrant laborers from different regions and different linguistic groups into close contact and cooperation with one another. From the earliest days of South Africa's gold and diamond rushes, mine managers had encouraged the practice of group dancing as a form of recreation for workers. Ethnic cultural tradition provided basic source material for the dances—which were typically performed in organized competitions—but, as David Coplan has argued, "the urban compound environment stimulated the creation of new patterns directly relevant to life in the mines."[93] Thus, as the plans for separate development began to take shape, the NP's minister of mines stressed the need for migrant workers to be "periodically returned to their homes to renew their tribal connections."[94] The modern industrial economy was simply too vast to be rigidly organized along tribal lines.

By the late 1970s, an attempt was made to repackage the urban Bantu councils as newly reformed community councils. Though all mention of tribal society and chieftaincy had been stripped away, the new councils retained key elements of indirect rule's basic design. Each of the council's powers—from the management of housing for migrant laborers, to the provision of local services—was directly connected either to the maintenance of apartheid "influx controls" or to the distribution of patronage resources intended to purchase legitimacy for the state.[95] As Robert Price suggests, had the councils succeeded at their task, "indirect rule—blacks controlling blacks—would then have been substituted for the coercive fist of the white state."[96] But by 1977, the year the Community Councils Act was introduced, the wave of domestic and international opposition that would finally destroy the apartheid state was already building momentum.

Separate development—the apartheid state's grandest and most preposterous contrivance—collapsed almost instantaneously as the transition to nonracial democracy began in 1990. A government publication from 1993 described its fate with a masterpiece of understatement:

Realities have shown that the linkage policy, whereby all blacks—including those living outside the self-governing territories—were ethnically linked to those states, did not satisfy black political aspirations.[97]

The extent of those aspirations is registered in the increasingly explosive political climate. Twenty political strikes were held in 1985, twenty-nine in 1986, compared with no more than five in any previous year. The number of armed attacks on government targets by resistance fighters tripled between 1981 and 1983 and again between 1984 and 1986, reaching a high of 230 in 1986, compared with four in 1976.[98] The homelands scheme ultimately failed to package political oppression and economic exploitation in a popularly legitimate form. But while the grander visions of separate development were downplayed after the 1970s, the ideological strategies of costuming and concealment soon found their way onto the urban battlefields of the insurrectionary 1980s.

3

Proxy Forces

The coercive powers of the state often appear as tools of last resort, to be deployed only when and where efforts at building consent fail. Like Max Weber, Antonio Gramsci rooted his reflections on political life in precisely this distinction:

> The methodological criterion on which our own study must be based is the following: that the supremacy of a social group manifests itself in two ways, as "domination" and as "intellectual and moral leadership." A social group dominates antagonistic groups, which it tends to "liquidate," or to subjugate perhaps even by armed force; it leads kindred and allied groups.[1]

But while consent and coercion may be analytically demarcated to useful effect, in the concrete apparatuses of the state and the practical world of political life, they are perpetually intertwined. Thus, while indirect rule and its descendants were premised on the search for legitimacy, their existence always assumed the availability and occasional use of coercive force. Chieftaincy could function as a form of substate under the wider regimes of colonial and segregationist rule not only because chiefs were assumed to be the bearers of a culturally given traditional authority (and assumed, therefore, to receive the automatic consent of their subjects), but because they were backed by homeguards, police officers, and military units. Yet, if indirect rule's primary objective was to win the consent of the governed, while also retaining a coercive capacity for use in emergencies, other forms of political apparatus might see the balance between consent and coercion reversed.

For over a decade after the rural rebellions in the Transkei and the forced exile of the ANC, PAC, and the South African Communist Party (SACP), the NP government appeared to have driven its opponents from the field. Not until the Durban strikes of 1973 was there any real indication that the apartheid state would face a significant political challenge from South Africa's disenfranchised majority. The Durban labor actions offered an early indication as to one of the key sites from which racial segregation would ultimately be overturned, but it was the 1976 student protest in Soweto that seemed to mark the beginning of apartheid's end. The Soweto rebellion began in June with a march by high school students protesting the introduction of Afrikaans as the language of instruction in black schools. The demonstrators were fired on by police, and the protest quickly escalated into a general confrontation, with students attacking police stations, government buildings, and state-run beer halls. By August, the leaders of the Soweto Student Representatives Council (SSRC) had made a decision to attempt to expand the political parameters of the protest by calling for a general work stoppage. The first such action was called on August 4 and was supported by about two-thirds of black workers in Johannesburg and Pretoria. The SSRC immediately began organizing for a second strike, scheduled to take place three weeks later.[2] Initial support for the second strike was estimated at about eighty percent. But as the action moved into its second day, events took a dramatic turn. Late in the afternoon, a group of between one thousand and fifteen hundred workers from the Mzimhlope hostel, armed with sticks, spears, and machetes, began moving through the streets of Soweto, attacking anyone in their path.[3]

Single-sex, dormitory-style hostels for migrant workers began to be developed on commercial farms and mine sites as early as the 1870s. In urban areas, migrant workers' hostels were constructed by both private firms and municipal governments to control the supply of labor to the manufacturing and construction industries. The choice of single-sex dormitory units over family housing was linked to the broader project of geographic racial segregation: black workers were considered to be temporary migrants to the cities, rather than permanent residents. As apartheid ideology increasingly fixated on tribal or ethnic identity, greater emphasis was placed on ensuring that hostel residents were housed along ethnic lines. The physical separation of the hostels from family housing in the surrounding townships, as well as the institutionalization of ethnic difference through the assignment of beds, gradually prepared the ground for a growing rift between migrant workers and township residents. Longtime township residents often perceived hostel men as backward foreigners competing with them for jobs. Hostel dwellers often perceived township residents as aloof, threatening strangers.[4]

There was at least one precedent for a violent confrontation between hostel men and township residents. In the fall of 1957, simmering tensions between young men from the Johannesburg township of Meadowlands and residents of the nearby Dube hostel escalated into conflicts in which thirty-three people died.[5] The clashes between men from the Mzimhlope hostel and Soweto residents resulted in a similar level of casualties. The fighting continued for two days, leaving thirty-one dead and hundreds injured.[6] The attacks were initially described in the press as "worker backlash against intimidation," with early explanations for the incident suggesting that men from the hostel had spontaneously retaliated against students trying to prevent them from going to work.[7] Yet, the extent of the attacks seemed to go well beyond a simple confrontation between demonstrating students and workers trying to get to their jobs. Rather than concentrating their attacks on the student demonstrators as a group, the hostel men seemed to target the community at large, smashing windows, breaking into houses, and generally assaulting residents.

As journalists continued to follow the story, ethnic conflict was put forward as a possible cause of the violence. Early press coverage of the incident specifically identified the hostel men as Zulus and described the attackers as a "massive *impi*," using the Zulu word for a military unit.[8] Some observers reported that the attackers shouted Inkatha slogans, identifying themselves with the Zulu cultural organization launched in 1975 under the aegis of the KwaZulu Bantustan administration.[9] Chief Mangosuthu Gatsha Buthelezi, leader of Inkatha and chief minister of KwaZulu, angrily denied that Inkatha was involved with the events at Mzimhlope and declared it "tribalist and racist" to suggest that Zulus alone were responsible for the attacks.[10] Closer to the events themselves, Inkatha's Transvaal-area representative, Gibson Thula, played a central role in attempting to mediate the conflict, arranging meetings between men from the hostel and student leaders.[11] Thula also reported that the hostel population was not monolithically Zulu, eroding the claim that ethnic tensions lay behind the clash. Further, census figures for 1970 showed Zulu-speakers to be the largest single ethnolinguistic group in the Soweto townships, accounting for thirty-three percent of the population.[12] Even if the attackers from the hostel had all been Zulu-speakers, many of their victims would have been as well.

Even more curious than the lack of any clear motive for a clash between township and hostel residents were the prophetic powers of the police. A full week before the beginning of the second strike and the outbreak of violence, Tsietsi Mashinini, chair of the SSRC, received a "friendly warning" from the police that he might wish to give himself up for his own protection from angry hostel dwellers.[13] As the strike date approached, Major-General Mike Geldenhuys, chief of the Johannesburg security police, warned in the press that political agitators in the townships would soon face a backlash from law-abiding citizens.[14] Just as the omens foretold, leaflets typed in Tswana and Zulu began to appear on Soweto streets, reading:

Tsotsis [gangsters] do not want us to go to work and they will beat us up if we board any transport into town. We are sick and tired of this nonsense and will defend ourselves. Let us take our kieries [clubs] and sticks and fight anybody who stops us. We are tired of people without brains. Signed, City Workers[15]

As the attacks began, the same police forces who had met student demonstrators with tear gas, bullets, and bird-shot, seemed helpless in the face of
the club-wielding hostel men. Reporters from the *Star* saw police in armored
vehicles, vans, and cars parked near the Mzimhlope hostel during the attacks
who took no action to contain or disperse the mob.[16] When asked to comment on the incident, General Prinsloo, the commissioner of police, seemed
to echo not only the spirit but the precise language of the "City Workers"
leaflet, saying, "I have no knowledge of these rampaging Zulus. But if it did
happen I'm not surprised. If people want to organize themselves into resisting the *tsotsis* we can't stop them."[17]

It might have appeared as though the residents of Soweto had spontaneously organized themselves to resist thuggery and intimidation, but the veil
of appearances would be pierced by a few well-placed journalists and photographers. The morning after the attacks began, the *Rand Daily Mail* published a
series of photographs taken outside the hostel. The first shows a group of black
men standing in front of an armored car being addressed by a white policeman
and a black interpreter through a loudspeaker. The second shows the men
turning and marching off, armed with sticks and clubs.[18] The next day, several
other photos were released showing white men in suits and camouflage
fatigues standing near the armed mobs.[19] One reporter for the *Rand Daily
Mail*, whose home happened to be near the hostel, had hidden himself in the
outdoor coal box during the first night of violence. According to his account,
in the early hours of August 25, police used a loudspeaker to warn the attackers that they had not been ordered to destroy property but "to fight people
only."[20] Police were also seen escorting a provisions truck into the area and dis-
tributing food to men from the hostel.[21] Although the responses of Buthelezi
and Gibson Thula to the attacks (in particular, Thula's dressing-down by the
police for his attempts to mediate the conflict) put Inkatha's role in the incident
into doubt, investigative journalists turned up allegations that T. J. Makhaya, a
senior Inkatha member and chairman of the Soweto Urban Bantu Council (a
partly appointed, partly elected advisory body modeled on the lines of the
homelands scheme) favored resisting the student activists with force.[22]

The repression of demonstrators, however, is a task better suited to police,
soldiers, courts, and prisons than to ragtag mobs of migrant workers. Thus,
while the NP government's decision to resort to coercive force during the
Soweto uprising is entirely unremarkable, the reasoning behind its choice of
coercive apparatus in the Mzimhlope incident is worthy of consideration.
Clearly, the availability of official repressive forces was not at issue. The initial student demonstrations had been put down in the expected manner,
with uniformed police and soldiers swinging the batons and firing the rifles.
But the intended purpose of the Mzimhlope attack went well beyond simply
clearing the streets of demonstrators, as the comments of Minister of Police
Jimmy Kruger suggested:

> As I see it, there is a struggle between the activists and their leadership against the proper, chosen leaders of the township whom the activists consider to be stooges. They are not stooges.[23]

Before the afternoon of August 24 there was no political struggle over the student mobilization that could be said to be wholly internal to the township community itself. There was indeed a lack of communication between the township activists and the hostel—even a social divide between the two communities—but no open confrontation.[24] The creation of such a conflict was precisely what the Mzimhlope attack was meant to achieve. The purpose of the proxy force was to costume an act of state coercion as an independent expression of community sentiment.

But an appropriate costume could not be created out of whole cloth. In order to appear as the representative of a particular community, the proxy must possess some plausible form of membership therein. The problem for a state seeking to employ a costumed proxy, then, is the source of a suitable candidate: easily recognizable as a member of the target community, yet willing to turn on it when necessary. For both indirect rule and the urban vigilante mob, a solution was found in the levering open of a preexisting line of social division. In the case of indirect rule, an existing or even imagined hereditary elite was partially severed from and redeployed against the rural peasantry. In the case of the Mzimhlope incident, a marginalized element of the proletariat was leveraged against student activists and their supporters. The process of widening a social division, however, always risks going too far. The proxy force (or its employer) must work constantly to renew its claim of identity with the target community; to prevent exposure of the contradiction between its content and its form.

"Black-on-Black Violence"

During the 1980s, South Africa's segregationist state made its last stand against both domestic and international opposition. In the black townships, civic associations founded in response to relatively minor local grievances began to make the jump into national struggles and radical politics. The black trade unions followed a similar trajectory, increasingly aligning themselves with a broad-based national political struggle. The ANC's simultaneous escalation of its armed struggle brought the country to the brink of revolution by the middle of the decade. Prior to the 1976 uprising, the black townships received little attention in the English and Afrikaans press. Ten years after Soweto school children shattered South Africa's seeming calm, violent clashes between vigilante groups, hostel residents, and rival political organizations would become regular daily events.

The broad dynamics of those clashes can be characterized by time period and family resemblance. In the middle 1980s, activists and supporters of the

United Democratic Front (UDF)—an umbrella organization of civic associations, student groups, and trade unions—found themselves under attack by
a variety of forces. In Natal, the UDF was confronted by Inkatha, with the
clashes between their supporters steadily escalating into what appeared to be
a racially segregated civil war. In the Eastern Cape, UDF activists were met by
an organization called Ama-Afrika. In the Orange Free State, civic association members were attacked and murdered by a vigilante squad known as
the A-Team. After the legalization of the ANC in 1990 and the opening of
negotiations for the country's first nonracial elections, the Natal violence
between Inkatha and the UDF appeared to spill over into the Transvaal Reef,
where hostel residents aligned to Inkatha battled ANC supporters in the surrounding townships, and commuter trains were the target of regular attacks
by gunmen. An extremely conservative estimate put the number of people
killed in "incidents of civil unrest" between 1984 and 1992 at over ten
thousand.[25]

Explaining the violence became the work of journalists and scholars, who,
by the time of the 1994 elections (and the sudden disappearance of much
of the violence), had thrown every conceivable social scientific paradigm
and method into the fray of newspaper columns, journal articles, and man-
uscripts. Ethnic conflict was an early favorite, especially among American
journalists. For several years, the *New York Times* featured such headlines as
"Tribal Feuds Won't Let Up in South Africa's East." Pull-quotes declared the
township conflicts to be driven by "an ethnic divide: the Zulus versus the
Xhosas."[26] Similar explanations of the violence were simultaneously on offer
from such credentialed academics as Hermann Giliomee, Donald L.
Horowitz, and Anthony Minnaar.[27] Others attributed the violence to political rivalry or local gangsterism.[28] The concept of "resource mobilization" was
employed as a highly overworked way of saying that people were using what
they had to get what they wanted.[29]

Most early explanations for the violence contained a similar set of glaring
oversights and fatal contradictions. In Natal, for example, where much of
the heaviest fighting took place, the black population was almost monolithically Zulu speaking. Organizing an ethnic conflict between members of the
same ethnolinguistic group would seem to have been difficult, at best. In the
townships of the Transvaal Reef, on the other hand, the especially high level
of ethnic diversity made it virtually impossible for the combatants to sort
themselves out neatly according to the language they spoke at home.[30] While
avoiding the contradictions of the ethnic explanations, the socioeconomic
models tended to take for granted the sudden availability of firearms
(including shotguns and assault rifles) and the relatively professional nature
of many of the attacks.[31] Why the sudden surge of mass violence using military weapons and tactics, when poverty and unemployment had been structural features of township life for decades?

That question could only be answered by looking beyond the paradigm of "black-on-black violence" and including in the picture the role of the government in organizing and directing the conflict. The first hard evidence of the part played by government forces in the violence came in the form of a videotape recorded in December 1990 by a television news crew, showing police using an armored car to aid Inkatha fighters during a battle in the Johannesburg township of Thokoza.[32] Six months later, the state began to hemorrhage defectors and incriminating documents. Nico Basson, an ex-South African Defence Force (SADF) officer who claimed to have run an operation in Namibia aimed at undermining the South West African People's Organization (SWAPO) before that country's 1989 elections, alleged that his old unit was now providing weapons, training, and direction to Inkatha.[33] Documents were then leaked detailing state funding of Inkatha organizing drives. After several Inkatha members came forward with claims of having received paramilitary training from the army, president F. W. de Klerk was forced to admit that at least 150 Inkatha fighters had been trained by the SADF at a camp in the Caprivi Strip.[34] It soon became clear that the explosion of violence was neither ethnic conflict nor simple gangsterism, but part of a carefully orchestrated campaign to destabilize the black townships as the country's transition to democracy began.

Total Strategy

The middle 1970s were worrying times for the defenders of racial segregation in South Africa. The end of colonial rule in Angola and Mozambique, the guerrilla war in Rhodesia, and the Soweto uprising at home were all read by NP leaders as signs of an impending assault on "the right of self-determination of the white nation" by the forces of global communism.[35] "Total strategy" (the term itself borrowed from French counterinsurgency theorist Andre Beaufre) was meant to coordinate state action in all areas of social life under the aegis of a National Security Management System.[36] An institutional framework for the new system was salvaged from the previously obscure State Security Council (SSC).

As a framework for policy, total strategy was intended to normalize South Africa's international profile, revitalize its economy, and undermine its domestic opponents. In pursuit of the latter goal, the NP elite became increasingly obsessed with theories of counterinsurgency. In 1977, as defense minister (soon to become prime minister) P. W. Botha was outlining the vision of total strategy, Helmoed-Romer Heitman, an SADF officer and military theorist, published an article in a South African military journal suggesting a variety of ways in which "extra-legal operations" could aid the counterinsurgency effort. Poisoned food and medical supplies or grenades rigged for instant detonation could be channeled secretly to opposition groups, eliminating some activists and sowing suspicion among others; false information could create mistrust of opposition leaders. Above all, Heitman emphasized, "such operations would need to be suitably disguised."[37] Yet, it is less than immediately evident why a government openly committed to a doctrine of racial segregation and willing to send soldiers against school-children in its defense might suddenly seems coy about its desire to do away with revolutionary activists and organizations.

As the NP prepared for battle, pamphlets based on John J. McCuen's *The Art of Counter-Revolutionary War*, were circulated among government officials. It was McCuen who, in 1966, had made famous the doctrine of "winning hearts and minds" that would guide certain elements of American strategy and tactics in Vietnam.[38] His approach to counterinsurgency suggested that the elimination of opposition groups was in itself insufficient to turn the tide of an insurrection. Once revolutionary organizations had been driven from the field, it would then be necessary to fill the resulting void with counterorganizations. As the NP's pamphlet argued, "The government must take the lead under all groups, classes, clubs, and societies with the organization of social, career, sport, education, medical, religious, and military activities."[39] Opposition groups would be replaced by counterorganizations capable of channeling potentially revolutionary energies in "safe" directions.

Yet, in an atmosphere already charged with popular opposition to apartheid, effective counterorganizations could hardly display their state sponsorship openly. Herein lay the importance of Heitman's disguise. In its most basic form, the costuming of coercion might permit the repression of dissent, while still allowing the state's hands to appear clean. It was this sort of invisible repression that author Steven Mufson had in mind when he described total strategy's National Security Management System as "a system without faces."[40] Yet, McCuen's principle of the counterorganization suggests that the system must have a face—that face, however, must be the people's own. As Frederick Engels recognized in *The Origin of the Family, Private Property, and the State*, the dynamics of class struggle necessitate the existence of state repressive apparatuses separate and distinct from the bulk of society.[41] To form an effective counterorganization, then, an appendage of the state must not simply conceal itself, it must retreat into its distant roots as a self-identical organization of the people. It is then visibility, not concealment, that becomes crucial. The costumed state apparatus must not only act, it must be seen to be "acting as"—claiming for itself the right of representation.

Proxy Operations

The Soweto rebellion had, indeed, only been a prelude to the insurrection of the 1980s. Yet, as the opposition dramatically escalated its struggle against apartheid, the state's response appeared curiously contradictory. On the one hand, states of emergency were declared in 1985 and 1986, reinforcing the powers of the police and military to enforce bans on political activity in the black townships. On the other hand, statistics compiled by the South African Institute of Race Relations reveal a decrease in the number of persons killed by government security forces after 1985. How could a widening insurrection and a clampdown by the state's repressive apparatuses result in fewer fatalities than before? The explanation for this seemingly counterintuitive finding lies in the simultaneous increase in the number of "unrest fatalities" described by the South African Bureau for Information as episodes of "black-on-black violence."[42] Within these figures, we can recognize the apartheid state's increasing reliance on a bizarre menagerie of proxy forces.

In many communities, these appeared—like the Mzimhlope hostel men—as local vigilante squads taking action against unruly elements. The Orange Free State townships of Thabong, Tumahole, and Seeisoville (in which rent and consumer boycotts had been organized by the UDF) were hit by sporadic violence centered around a group called the A-Team, whose leaders had vowed to "scour the township of rowdyism."[43] In the Cape Town squatter camps of Crossroads and KTC, UDF activists were attacked by amorphous groups calling themselves the *Amadoda* [men] or the *Otata* [fathers]. Many residents reported that during such clashes in January 1986, a white policeman fluent in Xhosa spoke to the *Otata*, reminding them of their traditions and their duty to rein in disrespectful youth.[44] In May 1986, the vast squatter settlements, which had successfully resisted several official removal orders, were reduced to ashes by a group known as the *Witdoeke*.[45] Within a month, forged UDF pamphlets appeared in the townships of the Eastern Cape announcing the impending collection of a monthly tax. These were followed by other pamphlets calling for the formation of anti-UDF groups along the lines of the Cape Town *Witdoeke*.[46]

Amidst the extreme poverty and high unemployment of the apartheid-era townships, it would take little more than a small amount of money, a few weapons, and promises of immunity from prosecution to mobilize an ad hoc vigilante squad. But the development of more durable counterorganizations to the UDF and ANC—the kind envisioned by McCuen's counterinsurgency strategy—required more significant commitments of resources, infrastructure, and personnel. In 1986, the South African Traditional Healers' Council (SATHCO) was founded with a loan of R300,000 from the man who would become the organization's secretary-general, "Pip" Erasmus. Erasmus was later revealed to be a former Rhodesian army counterintelligence agent who had been transferred to the SADF payroll. Traditional medicine is a sizable informal industry in South Africa (given the lack of access to standard medical care for most blacks during the apartheid era) and traditional healers make up part of the entrepreneurial sector of most township communities. Political guidance, however, was also available from the organization's leaders. Under the guise of a holistic approach to healing, a 1987 edition of the organization's newsletter, *Siyavuma*, noted that traditional health meant "total stability . . . there must not be disruptive elements like revolution."[47]

The institutional infrastructures for the more substantial counterorganizations were found in the Transkei, Ciskei, and KwaZulu homeland governments, as well as in front companies, such as Adult Education Consultants/Eduguide (AEC). The latter's existence as a proxy operation was revealed in 1992, when Dr. Ben Conradie, the director of its Eastern Cape branch, leaked several documents to the *Weekly Mail*.[48] The documents showed Lieutenant-General Rudolf Badenhorst, then the head of SADF military intelligence, signing official correspondence on behalf of AEC. The story was confirmed in 1994 by Lourens du Plessis, a colonel in the SADF who had been responsible for operations in the Eastern Cape during the 1980s.[49] Conradie revealed that in 1986 AEC had been responsible for Project Henry, an operation designed to oppose the UDF in Port Elizabeth with an African nationalist proxy organization to be headed by Rev. Ebenezer Maqina, who had recently been expelled from the Azanian People's Organization. Maqina was supplied with money and office equipment to found a group called Ama-Afrika, which quickly became known for the kidnapping, torture, and murder of UDF activists and supporters in Port Elizabeth and Uitenhage.[50] The accounts of these assaults are gruesome— people hacked to death with machetes, their heads split open with pick handles—and by their very nature tend to loom large in the remembrance of events. But we should also note what the SADF's military intelligence commanders took to be the central purpose of the operation: "to influence people to act in a certain way."[51]

Documents leaked to the press in 1993 by Bantu Holomisa, a general in the Transkei Defence Force, revealed that Maqina's group was ultimately meant to be incorporated into a grand scheme for the Eastern Cape known as Operation Katzen.[52] Referring to an order from the state president that the country's political situation be "normalized" by the end of 1986, Katzen's author(s) noted the following necessary considerations in the formulation of an appropriate strategy:

- The plan must entail minimum political risk for the RSA.
- Actions must not be traced back to the RSA.
- The Xhosa struggle for unity as a nation (particularly in Transkei) must be exploited or taken advantage of.
- There must be maximum use of traditional leaders.
- The present Ciskei Government must be replaced with a pro-RSA Government.[53]

The ensuing plan envisioned the establishment of a "Xhosa Resistance Movement" to be led by Charles Sebe (the brother and imprisoned rival of Ciskei leader Lennox Sebe[54]), which would act as "an independent power block against the ANC and UDF," and lay the basis for a unification of Transkei and Ciskei, "as the fatherland of the Xhosa wherever he finds himself."[55] Katzen's organizing principle was thus a reinvigoration of the Bantustan concept with the added twist of a seemingly independent ethnopolitical movement. The plan was put into motion in September 1986, when Charles Sebe was freed from a Ciskeian prison by men described in the press as mercenaries. Flyers announcing his leadership of the "Ilizo Lomzi Movement" briefly appeared, and in February 1987 the Transkei Defence Force launched an attack on Lennox Sebe's presidential palace.[56] The Xhosa Resistance Movement, however, turned out to be stillborn, and the operation either faded into embarrassed obscurity or was officially shelved.

Operation Katzen would appear to have been little more than the feverish brainstorm of a few counterinsurgency specialists were it not for one of their bibliographic references. The Katzen documents explicitly cited Inkatha as their working model, suggesting that the Eastern Cape operation was less a wild and impossible intrigue than a failed attempt to replicate a previous success.[57] Inkatha had for many years offered both journalists and scholars an irresistibly fascinating set of paradoxes: an organization intimately connected to the homelands system that declared itself opposed to apartheid; a Zulu cultural organization that also spoke in the language of black nationalism; a black political movement supposedly spared from official repression because of its commitment to nonviolence whose members were responsible for systematic, brutal attacks on their political rivals.[58] At the heart of these contradictions lay varying interpretations of Inkatha's relationship with the segregationist state. Lawrence Schlemmer and John Kane-Berman saw in Inkatha a moderate black opposition movement that might one day win a power-sharing agreement from the NP government. Roger Southall, Gerhard Mare, and Georgina Hamilton saw an opportunistic Bantustan elite advancing a petit bourgeois agenda through its collaboration with apartheid. An intriguingly suggestive interpretation was offered by Shula Marks, who saw in Buthelezi and Inkatha an ambiguous combination of opposition and collaboration, born of their dependence on the state. Between these three paradigms—opposition, collaboration, and dependence—only the last began to broach the question of Inkatha's existence as an independent entity. The bulk of academic work on Inkatha focused on its public presence: its actions, public documents, and leaders' rhetoric. What was naturally privileged by these interpretations was the organization's independent integrity. Inkatha's apparent independence, however, was an image consciously fostered by the apartheid state itself.

Inkatha was formally established in 1975 under the auspices of the KwaZulu Legislative Assembly (KLA). Its organizational roots, though, can be traced back at least a year earlier, to an organizing committee known as *Ubhoko*.[59] The earlier date corresponds with the claim made by Martin Dolinchek, a former officer in the Bureau of State Security (BOSS), that in 1974 an office was set up in Empangeni to carry out security and surveillance work through Inkatha.[60] It was also in 1974 that organized opposition to Buthelezi's leadership of KwaZulu appeared in the form of a party called *Umkhonto ka Shaka*, led by Chief Charles Hlengwa, deputy speaker of the KLA. Buthelezi had alleged that Hlengwa's challenge to his leadership was backed by Pretoria and produced as evidence a copy of a deposit slip transferring R12,000 from a BOSS agent to Hlengwa's bank account.[61] The incident had been widely assumed to signify the NP's frustration with Buthelezi's highly publicized refusal to accept the final stages of Bantustan independence for KwaZulu. According to Dolinchek, the operation had an additional aim: BOSS had indeed supported Hlengwa in setting up *Umkhonto ka Shaka*, but had then leaked the reports of payoffs and secret bank accounts in order to boost Buthelezi's credentials as an independent black nationalist.[62]

Links between BOSS and Inkatha also feature in the career of one of Buthelezi's longest-serving lieutenants, Melchizedec Zakhele "M. Z." Khumalo. Khumalo (Buthelezi's personal assistant in the 1980s) had been employed by the Department of Information, a government propaganda unit with close ties to BOSS, as early as 1963.[63] In the early 1970s, Khumalo was reportedly fired for passing information to Buthelezi, who in turn offered him a position in the KwaZulu department of agriculture. As with the original version of the *Umkhonto ka Shaka* episode, the curious element here is the government's exceedingly delicate treatment of Buthelezi and those around him. Had the state wished to bring Buthelezi back into line for his refusal of Bantustan independence or his claims of allegiance with the antiapartheid struggle, any number of sanctions could have been deployed against him, not the least of which would have been a tightening of the financial taps that kept the entire KwaZulu administrative system afloat. As for M. Z. Khumalo (whose name would appear again in dealings between Inkatha and the state in the 1980s), minor operatives who pass information to the opponents of highly repressive states are more often jailed or killed than allowed to make comfortable career transitions. The more likely possibility is that somewhere within the NP's security apparatus, someone had discovered a sharp, albeit useful, irony. If Buthelezi's criticism of separate development had provided him with the ability to speak not as a lackey of the government, but as a member of the liberation struggle, then his refusal of independence for KwaZulu was, in fact, what made him appear independent. Though he often seemed to flout the authority of the state, Buthelezi was a thoroughly serviceable tool. At times, it was precisely his apparent defiance that made for his usefulness.

The image of Inkatha's opposition to apartheid seemed to hold until the early 1980s. Patrick Lekota, a central figure in the UDF who was active in Natal, recalls that before 1983 Inkatha was widely regarded in the townships as the ANC in another guise.[64] Even after groups of Inkatha members began armed attacks on UDF supporters in 1985[65] it was still possible, Lekota suggests, to view the events as the result of tensions between two rival antiapartheid organizations:

> No one who did not know what they were going to do could have predicted that this thing was going to unfold in the manner that it unfolded. Because even when we had the fighting in Pietermaritzburg and so on, we thought it was just one incident as we might have in a normal situation. Now and then people's tempers are frayed and then, of course, they tackle each other. But I think we had not read the situation properly, as we were to discover later. Until then, we would not have anticipated that there was a plan to do what actually did happen.[66]

His reference is to the reports that began to appear in 1988, charging that Inkatha members had received paramilitary training from the SADF at a camp somewhere in KwaZulu.[67] These early accounts were corroborated in 1991 by Nico Basson, and in 1992 by Mbongeni Khumalo, a former leader of the Inkatha Youth Brigade and member of the organization's Central Committee. Khumalo stated that the 150 to 200 Inkatha members trained by the SADF were not, as President de Klerk had maintained following Basson's allegations, a VIP protection squad for the KwaZulu government, but a unit trained in assassination and guerrilla warfare for attacks on the UDF and ANC.[68] Khumalo also said he had witnessed a presentation to Inkatha's Central Committee by Dr. Louis Pasques, the president of AEC, proposing the formation of an Inkatha-led democracy movement drawing in such "moderate" groups as Ama-Afrika—a project for which some R11 million would be made available. Whether or not all of its leaders understood the full scope of the events in motion around them, Inkatha was being skillfully played as a central element in the state's strategy of counterrevolution by proxy.

The details were brought to light during the 1996 trial of former defense minister Magnus Malan, when a collection of documents was found inside a false fuse box in the home of Brigadier General Cornelius van Niekerk.[69] The documents recorded a series of meetings between Buthelezi and SADF officers and also included internal SADF correspondence regarding the creation of a paramilitary capacity for Inkatha under the code name Operation Marion. The earliest documents in the set show Buthelezi playing up his position as a valuable asset to the state, albeit one increasingly under threat.

A letter from Buthelezi to Admiral Dries Putter in November 1985 stated that he had frequently called for "the development of a paramilitary task force in KwaZulu," and that the situation was growing ever more critical with the growth of popular support for the UDF. Buthelezi's request was apparently acted on in February 1986 by a group of generals who agreed on a force of two hundred to be selected by Inkatha and trained by the army.[70]

The SADF's internal correspondence, however, suggests that the state intended to offer Buthelezi and Inkatha more than just a friendly helping hand. General Kat Liebenberg's formal report on the proposal described the paramilitary unit as, "A small full-time offensive element which can be used covertly against the UDF/ANC."[71] In the eyes of the SADF, the operation was not being executed with Inkatha, but through it. Thus, the minutes of a November 1989 meeting read: "Brig Buchner says Inkatha must not know that we choose targets. We must avoid the development of the perception that they are working for us."[72] Minutes of the State Security Council, produced later in the trial, reflect a similar sentiment. An appendix to the minutes of a February 1986 meeting notes that members of the SSC had been instructed to ensure that "support for Chief Minister Buthelezi . . . is kept clandestine to protect his image."[73] The careful management of imagery was, at times, planned down to the instruments with which it would be carried out. During one operation, Inkatha fighters were sent into the field with Russian-made weapons, to create the impression of a factional split within the UDF.[74] An even more ingenious variation on this theme involved arrangements with an armaments company for the manufacture of shotguns that would function effectively but would appear to be homemade. The weapons were then distributed to Inkatha fighters, bolstering their appearance as an independent political force.[75]

Inkatha's independence from the state was also meant to be enhanced by its entry into the field of trade unionism. Five months after the founding of the UDF-aligned Congress of South African Trade Unions (COSATU), a rival federation, the United Workers Union of South Africa (UWUSA), was formed under the patronage of Inkatha. At the time, Alec Erwin, a COSATU organizer and prominent Natal unionist, attributed the formation of UWUSA to a verbal attack on Inkatha made by Elijah Barayi, vice president of the National Union of Mineworkers at COSATU's launching rally. Whereas the unions had previously been cautious in their relations with Inkatha, Erwin argued, Barayi's promise to "bury Botha and Gatsha" had pushed Buthelezi to move against COSATU openly.[76] UWUSA quickly became known as a federation of sweetheart unions, due to the fact that its leadership was composed almost entirely of business owners and executives rather than workers.[77] But its existence as a state proxy was revealed in 1991, when several documents concerning Inkatha's relationship with the government were leaked to the press. The key document showed that in 1989

Minister of Law and Order Adriaan Vlok had ordered a commission of inquiry into UWUSA's viability, after the federation had run up huge debts despite receiving state funding of at least R1.5 million. Vlok's order questioned "how a project under the control of the SAP [South African Police] was allowed to develop in such a way" and stressed the concern that UWUSA's outstanding debts could eventually lead to the exposure of Project Omega, the counterinsurgency program under which it had been created. UWUSA remained active as a state-directed counterorganization as late as February 1990, when the federation was instructed to reserve Durban's Kings Park stadium for a mass meeting, preventing the ANC from holding a rally there following its legalization.[78]

It was in this transitional period, during the run-up to South Africa's first nonracial elections in April 1994, that the relationship between Inkatha and the NP government reached its most complex and unstable point. By the late 1980s, it had become clear that despite the bloody work of the counterinsurgency program, a political transition of some sort was inevitable. Yet, in its approach to the period of negotiations for a new constitution and nonracial elections, the NP continued to pursue the same stratagems of destabilization and counterorganization through the employment of proxy forces. One of Nico Basson's frequently reiterated charges was that the SADF's Namibian campaign against SWAPO had been explicitly conceived of as a test-run for an electoral contest between the NP and the ANC. The Namibian operation was aimed at minimizing support for SWAPO in the 1989 elections through the use of propaganda, assassinations, and the covert disruption of SWAPO-supporting communities by such means as the introduction of cholera into water supplies.[79] In February 1990, the SSC initiated a similar campaign in South Africa to "reduce the ANC to just another political party."[80]

Inkatha would figure prominently in that effort. In July 1990, the KwaZulu homeland government's cultural organization was formally relaunched as the Inkatha Freedom Party (IFP)—the public announcement of its detachment from the apparatuses of separate development setting the stage for a massive intensification of its covert support from the state. Two large Inkatha rallies were held in Durban prior to the IFP's birth. In advance of each, deposits of R100,000 and R150,000 were made to Inkatha accounts by the SAP.[81] In a memo from the Durban Regional Security Police to their national command, Major Louis Botha noted that it was "of cardinal importance" that arrangements be made to insure a large turnout at the March 1990 rally, "to show everyone that he [Buthelezi] has a strong base."[82] But that base was not to be built on rallies alone. In the days immediately following the March rally, more than 650 people were killed in fighting in the Pietermaritzburg area.[83] In August the conflict spread to the Johannesburg-area townships, where Inkatha fighters based in workers' hostels attacked residents in the surrounding townships and passengers on commuter trains. By mid-September, the official death toll neared seven hundred.[84] While Inkatha had made some organizing inroads in Soweto during the late 1970s, after the mid-1980s the organization could claim only marginal levels of support outside of rural Natal.[85] Thus, what was treated by the press and most academic observers as the escalation of an existing conflict was in fact its initiation.

In battle, the Inkatha forces identified themselves with red headbands. Representing either a clue to their concealed foundations or just a cruel joke of history, this was the same uniform worn by the Natal Native Contingent: Zulu soldiers drafted by the British to fight in their 1879 war with the Zulu kingdom. Though the lines were no longer drawn between colonial state and indigenous kingdom, Inkatha's soldiers remained the employees of a greater power. In preparation for the Johannesburg organizing drive, Themba Khoza and other Transvaal Inkatha leaders received a special training course from SADF military intelligence officers.[86] Larger numbers of Inkatha fighters were trained in urban combat by Springbok Patrols, a private security firm, and deployed in the fighting in Alexandra.[87] Larger numbers still were given a crash course in guerilla warfare at Mlaba camp in northern Natal.[88] As ANC members responded by organizing Self-Defence Units (often armed with AK-47s brought into the country by cadres of its military wing, *Umkhonto we Sizwe*), Inkatha fighters began to receive heavy weapons, including mortars and rocket grenades, from covert branches of the security police.[89] The ethnic antagonisms purported to be driving the violence were also the scripted product of state-run training camps. One IFP soldier interviewed by journalists about his experiences at a military camp commented: "We were taught about the Zulu kingdom and how to defend it." Another explained: "The Xhosas want to take our mineral resources to the Transkei. They've got nothing there. We will defend our kingdom."[90]

As the battles raged, the violence itself began to appear as an increasingly autonomous entity. In the press, in scholarly works, and in ordinary conversation, the violence came to be referred to as the work of the "Third Force." In this attribution lay the vague suggestion that the killings on the trains and in the townships were the work of some rogue covert element, connected neither to the government, nor its organized opponents. An occurrence of mass violence became proof in and of itself of the existence of this cabal of privatized assassins, former agents, and loose cannons bent on random, meaningless destruction. Of course, the eventual release of government memoranda and the testimony of security police operatives and military intelligence officers made clear that there was no such group with its own discrete existence, separate from the organs of the state. The violence was neither random in its direction nor meaningless in its intent, but a carefully scripted and staged production. The illusory autonomy of the Third Force was thus rooted not in an explanation, but in a failure to explain; its social reality finding a foundation in the only partially successful concealment of the state's coercive apparatus. Failure also stood behind the birth of Inkatha's true autonomy. The political space that would come to be occupied by the IFP in postapartheid politics could only open as the NP's dreams of stabilizing and normalizing its rule were foreclosed.

Inkatha's trajectory, then, traces the paradoxical path of the proxy force from ideological strategy to social reality. The proxy is meant to appear independent, but never to be so. Its discrete existence is intended to remain permanently illusory; its form as an autonomous force can never correspond with its structural reality as the agent of another. It is only when the lights are shut off and the technicians go home—or rather when the checks are no longer deposited and the supply of ammunition dries up—that the entity whose independent existence was only in the minds of the audience fades forever or begins to walk on its own. The paradox lies in the fact that the ability of the proxy force to transform its illusory autonomy into the genuine item seems to flow from the directing agency's investment in the proxy's image. A point is reached at which the collection of props and actors becomes so large that despite the departure of the producer and director, the show itself goes on.

4

Tradition and Modernity in the Fall of Apartheid

The British Colonial Office's postwar optimism about the end of indirect rule and the development of modern political institutions in Africa was echoed and amplified by the mainstream of professional political scientists across the Atlantic. Studies of transitional states and societies were very much in vogue for American political science departments during the 1950s and 1960s, as was the adoption of a neo-Weberian analytic framework—albeit one carefully expunged of all traces of hesitation about bureaucracy and rationalization. From Weber, American political scientists adopted both the concept of a historical transition from tradition to modernity and the notion of a corresponding shift in a society's form of legitimate authority.

As a result, modernization studies of sub-Saharan Africa tended to highlight transformations of the institution of chieftaincy. Where independent African states were emerging from colonial rule, the process of modernization was expected to involve the outright replacement of traditional authorities with modern bureaucratic administrators. Where a colonial power still remained, researchers seeking to apply the Weberian paradigm were faced with the apparent coexistence of both traditional and modern forms of authority. Studies such as Lloyd Fallers's *Bantu Bureaucracy*, A. K. H. Weinrich's *Chiefs and Councils in Rhodesia*, and J. F. Holleman's *Chief, Council, and Commissioner* accounted for indirect rule as the bureaucratization of traditional authority, envisioning chiefs as occupying a middling position between tradition and modernity.[1] The resulting clashes between competing bases of legitimacy were referred to in these studies and others like them as episodes of "role conflict." As Fallers described the situation:

> The tension between the introduced bureaucratic civil service pattern and the more particularistic traditional authority structures has produced different kinds of conflict at different levels within the political system. . . . Thus the chief is faced almost daily with conflicting expectations on the part of persons with whom he

interacts. Furthermore, the sanctions which operate in support of the two sets of norms are such as to leave him a very small margin of error in his attempts to balance the two sets of expectations.[2]

Rather than shifting African societies from the belief in hereditary rule to respect for rationalized bureaucracy, indirect rule was designed to bolster the material powers of the later by cloaking itself in the imagery of the former. But despite the long-standing investment of colonial power in traditional authority, some analysts continued to define tradition and modernity as mutually exclusive stages of social development. As modern European patterns of political authority failed to emerge in Africa's newly independent states, the suggestion was floated that a sort of neotraditional legitimacy now upheld the postcolonial regimes. "The concept of chieftaincy," David Apter proposed, "is the essence of the African personality."[3]

In this respect, as compared with the rest of sub-Saharan Africa, South Africa presented something of a paradox. On the one hand, by the middle of the twentieth century, the vast majority of the country's economic and political infrastructure had been thoroughly modernized. On the other hand, though, indirect rule had deliberately fostered segregated enclaves within which traditional authority was meant to thrive. Thus, as the final battles over de jure segregation were fought out, the status and future of chieftaincy were critical questions not only for the apartheid state, but for the organizations and leaders who hoped to succeed it. The leaders of Inkatha—occupying a station within the system of separate development, though clearly aspiring to a more substantial position of power—were best positioned to recognize and to make use of the institutions and ideologies of traditionalism, but often failed to do so. The ANC had flirted with traditionalist rhetoric in its early years, but by the 1950s had become thoroughly modernist in its internal structure and outlook. Yet, as the combined effects of domestic insurgency and international isolation finally brought about a negotiated transition to nonracial democracy, both organizations suddenly found it necessary to rethink their relationships to the institutions of chieftaincy.

Inkatha

The elaborate edifice of the Bantustan system was premised on a fusion of tribal traditionalism and African nationalism. Each, of course, had been interpreted and modified to fit the specific requirements of the apartheid state: "tribal tradition" as the institutions descended from generations of indirect rule; "African nationalism" as the call for a reinvigorated system of racial segregation. Accordingly, chiefs occupied important positions in the Bantustan administrative apparatuses, governing their local communities as well as occupying, in many cases, reserved majority seats in their homeland legislative assemblies. As a product of separate development, Inkatha could hardly have avoided multiple connections to the institution of chieftaincy. The organization's first constitution made all members of the KLA members of Inkatha at a stroke.[4] At the organization's inaugural meeting in 1975, eighteen of KwaZulu's twenty-six tribal authorities were represented.[5] If for no other reason, then, chiefs in KwaZulu would make up a significant constituency within Inkatha, simply by virtue of their dominant position in the KLA.

But chiefs in KwaZulu were not only Inkatha members by default—a sort of guaranteed membership intended to fill out the empty chairs. On the contrary, it was the chiefs themselves whose job it was to ensure that Inkatha took hold among the rural masses. In rural KwaZulu, Inkatha branches were organized so as to correspond with the boundaries of tribal authorities, and chiefs were expected to play a leading role in shepherding their subjects into the organization.[6] The degree to which they did so on an entirely consensual basis is unclear. The potential for coercion was certainly high. Bantustan residents, often women whose main source of income was an absent male family member engaged in migrant labor, were heavily dependent on the resources that flowed through the authority of the chief. Land, housing, and work permits all became easier to obtain when one was in the good graces of both the local chief and Inkatha.[7] At times, the chiefs themselves competed with one another to impress the KLA with the number of Inkatha members signed up in their areas.[8] Ultimately, of course, any benefits distributed by chiefs to their subjects came via the authority of the KLA. Bantustan chiefs thus took up a vital middling position in a patronage chain, standing as the active nexus between the homeland administration and the rural population. As a product and integral component of the homeland structure in KwaZulu, Inkatha drew its organizational strength and authority from this patron-client network and, thus, from the chiefs who oversaw its day-to-day operation.

Inkatha was never far removed from the power structures of indirect rule traditionalism, nor did it avoid traditionalism's rhetoric and imagery. As the leader of both Inkatha and its Bantustan base, Mangosuthu Buthelezi was known to sing the praises of Zulu traditional authority, writing in 1974:

> We will preserve the traditional system of Chieftainship in KwaZulu and re-affirm our constitutional relationship with the Paramount Chief and will build our future state with due regard to our cultural heritage and traditions adapted and fructified by the ideals of Western civilization and democracy and modern scientific principles.[9]

In 1957, Buthelezi was officially installed as chief of a tribal authority in Northern Natal and frequently claimed for himself hereditary status as "traditional prime minister" to the Zulu king.[10] Yet, it was precisely in the relationship between Buthelezi and the Zulu king, Goodwill Zwelithini, that the contradictory nature of Inkatha's traditionalism became most apparent. In 1971, when Zwelithini was officially inaugurated as king by the South African government, rumors were rife that he would be given some measure of executive authority within the KwaZulu homeland—a plan supported, for obvious reasons, by several members of the Zulu royal family.[11] When the reins of power were left in Buthelezi's hands, Zwelithini became something of a rallying figure for several attempts at launching opposition to Buthelezi's leadership of KwaZulu.

In 1972, the first of these efforts, Lloyd Ndaba's Zulu National Party, promised to raise Zwelithini to the status enjoyed by the Swazi king, that of a monarch with executive powers.[12] Two years later, Zwelithini's name was similarly employed by Charles Hlengwa's *Umkhonto ka Shaka*, although the king quickly distanced himself from the party when rumors of its connections to the Bureau of State Security were leaked.[13] During the intervening year it was alleged in the KLA that Zwelithini had sent a petition to the minister of Bantu administration requesting that Buthelezi be suspended.[14] Following the *Umkhonto ka Shaka* episode, Zwelithini pledged his support for Buthelezi in the press, but the chief minister demanded more. In January 1976, Zwelithini signed an oath pledging to refrain from "participation in any form of politics and from any action or words which could possibly be interpreted as participation in politics."[15] In 1979, the KLA voted to reduce the king's annual salary from R21,000 to R8,000, following charges that Zwelithini had violated the terms of his agreement by conspiring to form yet another opposition party, *Inala*. Once again, Zwelithini promised to hold his tongue and the money was restored.[16] If any question still remained as to the nature of the relationship between the Zulu king and his traditional prime minister, one always could consult the textbooks produced by an Inkatha-affiliated teachers' organization for use in all KwaZulu schools.[17] The texts consistently invert the order of importance between the king and his prime minister, placing Buthelezi (as the leader of Inkatha) in the position of paramount importance.[18]

Buthelezi's position within the KwaZulu hierarchy earned him considerable status and a luxurious standard of living. Yet, his sights were fixed significantly higher than the post of Bantustan chief minister. In the wake of the Soweto uprising, it became more and more widely assumed that apartheid would not last forever, and as speculation about a new political dispensation circulated, Buthelezi began to present himself and Inkatha as the leader and the organization through which a settlement could be delivered. During the Mzimhlope crisis, Buthelezi had attempted to build an image for himself as a black nationalist, stating in interviews that Inkatha's goals were the same as those of the Black Consciousness Movement and calling on blacks to unite across tribal lines against oppression.[19] Black Consciousness had originated in the late 1960s within the small but influential community of black university students. Steven Biko and other black student activists, frustrated by the moderate political stance of the multiracial National Union of South African Students, founded the racially exclusive South African Students' Organization (SASO) in 1969.[20] SASO became the base from which a new antiapartheid ideology would be developed, stressing the need for blacks (now broadly defined by the movement as inclusive of all those not race-classified as white) to reshape their social, psychological, and cultural identities. In its early years, Black Consciousness ideology was interpreted by some NP intellectuals as a position wholly compatible with the goals of separate development.[21] But after 1976, as Black Consciousness leaders declared their militant opposition to apartheid, a firm line of demarcation was drawn: Biko was arrested and murdered in police custody, while Buthelezi remained free and unmolested.

On the one hand, Buthelezi's public appearance as an opposition leader made him a useful proxy for the state. On the other hand, though, it is clear from his maneuvering behind the scenes that Buthelezi was interested in testing and transcending the limits of that role. In 1977, Buthelezi moved to open Inkatha membership to all African ethnolinguistic groups, replacing references to "Zulu" in the organization's constitution with the term "Black." Sensing a threat to the fundamental principles of separate development, Buthelezi was called to the office of Justice Minister Kruger, where the following exchange took place:

> Mr. Kruger: Don't you consider the Zulus as an entity on their own, as an entity of people I mean. What is the position between you and the Xhosas for example?
>
> Chief Buthelezi: No, I would say that the position between us and the Xhosas is the same as between the Afrikaners and the English. I mean they are all, you are the same people, as we are the same people. We have been speaking the same language in fact as the Xhosas.
>
> Mr. Kruger: But surely, Chief, you consider the Zulu people to be an independent people, an independent people in the sense that they are independent of other peoples, that you are a nation, a Zulu nation.
>
> Chief Buthelezi: Once we were conquered by the British of course, that fizzled away and once the whites of South Africa in 1910 decided to submerge us with all the other people of South Africa, it was not our decision.[22]

Buthelezi's statements about other ethnic groups were not always so gracious.[23] But for the ethnic entrepreneur who had reached the top of his profession, there remained only one road open to further advancement: a swift leap from the leadership of an ethnic homeland to that of a multiethnic race.

That leap was never truly made. Yet, Inkatha's desire to transcend the boundaries of the Bantustan continued to echo throughout the 1970s and 1980s. In discussing the identity and destiny of the nation, for example, Inkatha's school curriculum oscillated between concepts of ethnicity and race. While one text defined the term "nation" to mean "people of the same race who also share the same skin colour," another stated, "We are a Zulu nation. We don't doubt ourselves. We are proud of being Zulu."[24] If there was any respect in which the concepts of ethnicity and race came into resolution within the wider category of nationhood, it was in the imagery associated with the historical figure of Shaka. In Inkatha's school texts, the *Mfecane* was interpreted not as an imperialist conquest, but as an expression of Shaka's benevolent desire to unite all African ethnic groups.[25] The implied conclusion puts Inkatha in Shaka's place: leading the Zulu nation while uniting the black nation. Here, the texts drew a sharp contrast between Inkatha's ethnic/racial nationalism and the position of non-racialism staked out by the ANC in the 1980s:

> There are fellow Africans who have convinced themselves that any organization that is solely run by Africans, without whites, Indians or Coloureds, will not succeed. Such an attitude displays an inferiority complex in these Africans caused by many years of oppression by whites. There are many people who do not join organizations led by their own African people. They rather choose to go and seek refuge in organizations of other race groups. This is the type of action we must never ever contemplate taking. We must at all times join organizations of our own people first, even before thinking about organizations of other races. . . . A person with *ubuntu* [humanity] and pride of his/her nationality is the one who throws in his/her lot with organizations of their own people.[26]

But the Inkatha of the insurrectionary years was not always so scrupulous about the line of demarcation between itself and the ANC. At times, Inkatha leaders suggested that their organization not only worked toward the overturning of apartheid, but was in fact an internal wing of the exiled ANC. As Inkatha's former-secretary general Oscar Dhlomo suggested in 1984:

> In Inkatha circles the so-called ANC is officially referred to as the External Mission of the ANC. This is so because according to recorded history the external mission of the ANC in the person of the current caretaker of that movement, Mr. Oliver Tambo, was sent overseas by the last constitutionally elected President of the ANC, the late Chief Albert Luthuli, to drum up support for the liberation struggle of black people inside South Africa. There was never any intention that the external mission of the ANC would eventually develop a completely autonomous movement that would be free to decide on any liberatory strategies that would implicate millions of black people inside the country, without first consulting them.[27]

Accordingly, Inkatha adopted for itself the ANC's colors (black, green, and gold) as well as khaki uniforms similar to those worn by *Umkhonto we Sizwe* combatants.[28] The same colors graced the cover of an Inkatha publication reproducing letters from leaders of the ANC and the Black Consciousness Movement to Buthelezi. The letters are little more than polite communications—a sympathy note from Nelson Mandela following the death of King Cyprian, an invitation from Steven Biko to a South African Students' Organization conference—but the intent behind their collection and publication was made clear in the pamphlet's introduction:

> Inkatha is an expression of the same forces which brought the ANC into prominence in the late 50's and early 60's. The President of Inkatha was himself a member of the ANC Youth Wing when it was able to operate legally in the country. . . . There is a lot of vicious propaganda being circulated abroad by the UDF regarding the way in which the President of Inkatha is viewed by certain Black leaders. The UDF is attempting this tactic in order to appear to be closer to the ideals of the founding fathers of the African National Congress than Inkatha is.[29]

Perhaps the clearest indication of Buthelezi's desire to transform Inkatha into a black nationalist front came in the course of the Indaba negotiations in Natal during the middle 1980s. The origins of the Indaba lay in a 1979 government proposal to consolidate several disconnected patches of the KwaZulu homeland into something that might look more like a single geographic entity.[30] The South African Sugar Association, concerned that white-owned farmland might be appropriated in the process, commissioned Professor Jan Lombard to produce a study offering an alternate solution. Lombard apparently went far beyond the call of duty, proposing in the report much more than a simple redrawing of the Bantustan's boundaries. The report identified KwaZulu, rural Natal, and the Durban/ Pietermaritzburg metropolitan area as "distinct economic, cultural, and political configurations," from which an entirely new constitutional dispensation could be built.[31] The sugar industry was apparently unimpressed, as was the NP government.[32] Chief Buthelezi, however, reacted to the publication of the Lombard Report by forming his own commission to study the possibilities for a new political order in Natal. The commission's members included representatives from the largest capital interests in the region (Anglo-American Corporation, the Institute of Bankers, and the South African Cane Growers Association), members of Inkatha, and the KwaZulu Development Corporation, as well as political scientists Heribert Adam, Herman Giliomee, Lawrence Schlemmer, and Arendt Lijphart. The commission's final report was premised on the notion that Natal comprised one rather than two economic entities, and that certain of the artificial divisions between white and black areas of the region were responsible for economic inefficiencies that were now hindering development.[33]

In proposing a solution to the problem, however, the commission centered its analysis on the concept of cultural conflict, its recommendations corresponding closely with Arendt Lijphart's consociational paradigm. For Lijphart, an electoral democracy is forever doomed to reproduce preexisting lines of social consensus or division.[34] These, for Lijphart are primarily cultural: ethnolinguistic or religious in his favored Western European example of the Swiss canton system, but clearly racial in his recommendations for South Africa. The keys to political stability in a multicultural society are said, therefore, to lie in government by a grand coalition of elites representing each cultural entity and a high degree of autonomy for each group with regard to its own internal affairs. The Buthelezi Commission Report, then, called for Natal's legislative assembly to include guaranteed levels of representation for "communities of interest" and an executive formed by representatives of South Africa's four legally defined racial groups.[35]

The NP government summarily dismissed the Commission's report, as it had the Lombard plan, but after three years of insurrectionary struggle, the idea of a regional political experiment began to generate interest again. In April 1986, the KwaZulu/Natal Indaba was convened as a series of formal discussions between the governments of the KwaZulu homeland and the Province of Natal (along with several chambers of commerce, business organizations, and legal political parties[36]) on the subject of a new regional political dispensation. As had been the case in the previous exercises, consociationalism was the favored political paradigm. A bicameral legislature was proposed, one house to be elected through proportional representation, the other to be composed of race group representatives. A member of each racial group would also be represented in the region's executive.[37] Inkatha's support for the model of government proposed at the Indaba is notable for its acceptance of the principle of racial (rather than ethnic/tribal) representation. Although blacks in the Natal region were overwhelmingly Zulu-speakers, a move away from the legal assignment of political representation based on an ethnolinguistic category represented a clear departure from the NP's paradigm of separate development. As he had in 1977, when Inkatha was opened to multiethnic membership, Buthelezi was publicly proclaiming himself to be a leader not only of Zulu-speakers, but of black South Africans across ethnic lines.

Notably, in the final report of the Buthelezi Commission, nothing was said regarding the political role to be played by chiefs or the social status of traditional authority. Likewise, at the Indaba, the role of chiefs as political authorities was apparently never an issue of any importance. A small number of chiefs (between eight and twelve) were to be included in councils that would be consulted on legislation affecting the "cultural rights" of an officially recognized group,[38] but this lay a considerable distance from legislative or executive power. Correspondingly, the Indaba recommended the opening of freehold land rights to blacks. Under the systems of indirect rule and their apartheid-era variants, land in black rural areas was held in trust by a chief for the members of his community. The conversion to freehold land tenure in KwaZulu would have dramatically undermined the material basis of chieftaincy, leaving only its cultural afterimage in place.

For the Inkatha of the middle 1980s, however, the material powers of the chieftaincy could be willingly done away with, when and where those powers were soon to be replaced by modern forms of political authority. Indirect rule had sought to remake chieftaincy as a means to an end: cultural legitimacy would deliver automatic obedience. Whether or not the leaders of the KwaZulu homeland administration ever fully believed in the cultural power of traditional authority, they surely believed in and depended upon its material powers. If modernity promised to deliver an effective means of authority, cultural legitimacy could be quickly and easily forgotten.

The ANC

In its 1919 constitution, the South African Native National Congress offered ex officio membership to all hereditary chiefs, granting them the right to attend any of its functions and declaring that at such events a "separate place of honor" should be set aside for them.[39] But by the late 1950s and the NP government's passage of the Promotion of Bantu Self-Government Act, the ANC was speaking in the voice of an unalloyed modernism, declaring chieftaincy to be part of a historical stage now long past. As Nelson Mandela made the case in 1959:

> The Nationalists say that chiefs, not elected legislatures, are "the Bantu tradition." There was a time when, like all peoples on earth, Africans conducted their simple communities through chiefs, advised by tribal councils and mass meetings of the people. In those times the chiefs were indeed representative governors. Nowhere, however, have such institutions survived the complexities of modern industrial civilization.[40]

Identical sentiments were expressed by Govan Mbeki in his account of the resistance to the Bantu Authorities Act in the Transkei. For Mbeki, a member of both the ANC and SACP, a historical critique of the institution of chieftaincy was a direct application of Marxist theory as it was widely interpreted in the 1950s and 1960s. Particular social institutions belonged to particular stages of history. Thus, as Mbeki argued, "when a people have developed to a stage that discards chieftainship, when their social development contradicts the need for such an institution, then to force it on them is not liberation but enslavement."[41]

There is reason to believe, however, that Mandela and Mbeki were not always of the same mind on the question of the ANC's approach to the institutions of separate development and traditional authority. A long-running and extremely divisive debate between ANC leaders imprisoned on Robben Island was set off in the late 1960s by the question of whether or not to support an opposition candidate to Chief Kaiser Matanzima in the Transkeian elections.[42] Mandela favored engaging in the process; Mbeki opposed it. According to a document smuggled out of Robben Island in 1975, the debate went on for some six years and threatened at times to compromise Mandela's leadership of the group of jailed resistance fighters.[43]

There can be no question about the fact that during the first two decades of the apartheid state's attempt to establish the Bantustan system, the ANC's public position toward the institutions of separate development was one of unequivocal criticism and rejection. Such a position was entirely consistent with the organization's long-standing rejection of tribal or ethnic factionalism and its undeniably modernist assertion of multiethnic (and eventually nonracial) nationalism. At times, the extreme skepticism with which ANC cadres met the NP's enthusiasm for tribal identification bordered on fear of an international conspiracy.[44] The enhanced status and powers of chieftaincy inside the Bantustans were met with similar scorn. A 1969 issue of the ANC's journal, *Sechaba*, labeled the arbitrary authority held by chiefs over the allocation of land and the gathering of wood and thatching grass a form of rule "by means of terror."[45] Yet, the public rejection of separate development did not completely exhaust the ANC's consideration of the questions it raised. Behind the scenes, ANC leaders continued to explore the possibility of some level of engagement with the Bantustan governments.

While in 1969, the ANC's Morogoro Conference adopted a formal statement of strategy and tactics calling for an uncompromising revolutionary challenge to the institutions of apartheid, a decision was quietly taken to maintain contact with certain Bantustan elites who were thought to maintain genuine antiapartheid sentiments: Sabata Dalindyebo in the Transkei and Buthelezi in KwaZulu.[46] In 1979, a formal meeting between ANC and Inkatha leaders was arranged at the ANC's offices in London. According to a speech made by ANC president Oliver Tambo in 1985, the meeting was intended to have remained confidential—a decision consistent with the ANC's strategy of quietly inviting those within the system to join the liberation struggle.[47] Buthelezi's interests, however, seem to have been better served by an open meeting at which he could appear publicly as a resistance leader. The press was tipped off, leading to a long breach in relations between the two organizations.[48]

The strategy of quiet engagement with those inside the Bantustan system appears to have been shelved for several years following the 1979 debacle. But the question was revived during the ANC's 1985 Consultative Conference, when it was suggested from the floor during a plenary on strategy and tactics that some chiefs might be encouraged to play a role in the antiapartheid movement. A recommendation was adopted by the conference that "our approach and attitude towards traditional leaders should differentiate between puppet and patriotic traditional leaders."[49] The timing of the recommendation corresponded with a renewed drive inside South Africa by the UDF to extend antiapartheid organizing into the rural areas.[50] R. S. Ndou, a unionist and UDF activist in the 1980s (who would later become a central figure in the organized entrance of chiefs into the liberation struggle), recalled that early efforts by the UDF's rural desk were hindered by the fact that most UDF members were urbanites, unfamiliar with rural village communities.[51] Yet, with some forty percent of South Africa's black population living in rural areas, a means had to be found to reach them. According to Ndou, himself the son of a Venda chief and the product of a rural upbringing, the suggestion that rural organizers might attempt to make new inroads by first winning over the chiefs came from Oliver Tambo.[52] In 1986, during the popular resistance to the granting of Bantustan independence to KwaNdebele, an opportunity to put Tambo's plan into action seemed to present itself.

KwaNdebele, the last of South Africa's ten ethnic homelands to be cobbled together, held no relation to the territorial history of Ndebele-speakers as a group, but was instead the product of a successful lobbying effort by a cabal of ethnic entrepreneurs who recognized in the homelands scheme an opportunity for self-promotion. In the late 1960s, a group calling itself the Ndebele National Organization approached the government with a request for a homeland. Pretoria was only too happy to provide it, hoping to further the new policy of separate development. The first steps were taken in 1974, when the Ndzundza tribal authority was elevated to regional status. By 1980, a legislative assembly had been erected for the new self-governing state of KwaNdebele. The assembly's appointed seats were soon filled by the members of the Ndebele National Organization, with one of its leaders, S. S. Skosana, becoming the homeland's chief minister.

Unlike the other Bantustan governments, the forty-six member KwaNdebele legislative assembly included no chiefs. It soon became apparent, however, that this anomaly was the result of a power struggle, rather than an oversight.[53] Three years after its inception, the KwaNdebele government formed a separate body for chiefs, *Ibandla Lamakhosi*, ostensibly to honor their positions and keep them well above the dirty business of politics. Several chiefs, however, interpreted the move as an attempt to sideline them. In 1985, when it was announced that KwaNdebele would soon be granted independent status (and would in the process incorporate the border areas of Moutse and Ekangala), several chiefs threw in their lot with local residents protesting the plan. The resulting clash between the legislative assembly—backed by a large squad of vigilantes—and those opposed to an extension of the Bantustan was sufficiently bloody and destabilizing that the legislative assembly's petition for independence was eventually rejected by the government.

Seeking to restore the necessary image of stability, a police crackdown began against KwaNdebele's dissident chiefs.

Several refugees from the KwaNdebele struggle found their way to Johannesburg and the UDF cadres operating out of COSATU's headquarters. There, the groundwork was laid for the formation of a UDF affiliate to be known as the Congress of Traditional Leaders of South Africa (CONTRALESA). Following a series of small, covert meetings with sympathetic chiefs from KwaNdebele and Lebowa, CONTRALESA's existence was announced publicly at a press conference in September 1987.[54] The organization's leaders stated their commitment to the continuing struggle over KwaNdebele, but declared their long-term objective to be "the eradication of the Bantustan system."[55] Similar sentiments were expressed in a joint communiqué issued by CONTRALESA and the ANC following a meeting at the ANC's headquarters in Lusaka, Zambia:

> Our traditional leaders feel very keenly the effects of the apartheid system. The very institution of chieftainship has been overturned and abused by the racist rulers. From leaders responsible and responsive to the people, you are being forced by the regime to become its paid agents. From being a force for unity and prosperity you are turned into perpetrators of division, poverty and want among the oppressed.
>
> Dear compatriots! Dear traditional leaders!
>
> You have an important role to play NOW in the struggle against apartheid. Your place is in the front ranks of the mass democratic offensive. Let us together shape the future South Africa in which justice, peace and prosperity will reign.[56]

There can be no question about the nature of CONTRALESA's stance vis-à-vis the apartheid system in the late 1980s. But it is precisely the organization's antiapartheid stance and rhetoric that seem to obscure the question of its own conception of the nature and role of traditional authority. To the extent that the institution of chieftaincy had become part and parcel of the Bantustan apparatus, CONTRALESA called for chiefs to abandon their positions and become freedom fighters in a mass democratic movement. Yet, there was simultaneously an extent to which that appeal spoke to chiefs as "traditional authorities," drawing a distinction between the institutions of indirect rule and their buried, "authentic" incarnations. Whether this ambiguity had any effect on the participation of CONTRALESA-aligned chiefs in the antiapartheid struggle is unclear. Where it promised to take on a much greater salience, though, was in the question of the role to be played by chiefs in a postapartheid South Africa. If, through their participation in the liberation struggle, chiefs were liberating themselves from an authoritarian institution—becoming democrats and egalitarians rather than rural autocrats—then, in a liberated South Africa, chieftaincy would presumably disappear. If, however, it was not the individuals within the institution, but the institution itself that was to be mobilized in support of the struggle, then chieftaincy could be expected to survive the transition intact; shifting its allegiance perhaps, but not its form.

In its 1988 *Constitutional Guidelines for a Democratic South Africa*, the ANC addressed the question of postapartheid chieftaincy directly, calling for the institution to be "transformed . . . in conformity with the democratic principles embodied in the constitution."[57] Where chieftaincy and electoral democracy did not meet eye to eye, it was the former that would be expected to make way. Yet, within four years and the opening of negotiations for the transition to electoral democracy, the strong language referring to a transformation of the institution of chieftaincy had been shelved. In its place was a delicately worded effort at accommodation:

> The institution of chieftainship has played an important role in the history of our country and chiefs will continue to have an important role to play in unifying our people and performing ceremonial and other functions allocated to them by law. The powers of chiefs shall always be exercised subject to the provisions of the constitution and other laws. Provision will be made for an appropriate structure consisting of traditional leaders to be created by law, in order to advise parliament on matters relevant to customary law and other matters relating to the powers and functions of chiefs. Changes in the existing powers and functions of chiefs will only be made by parliament after such consultation has taken place.[58]

During Inkatha's moment of ambition at the Indaba, the tradition that seemed to matter most had been the tradition of power. As the ANC prepared for its endgame with the apartheid state, the power of tradition had become a sudden and pressing concern. Why had this seemingly marginal issue now loomed large? The answer could be found in the name that had been given to the radically transformative approach to rural chieftaincy: "The Mozambican Option."

RENAMO and the Reflux of Tradition

As in the British colony of Natal, Portuguese colonial administration in Mozambique followed the model of indirect rule. Mozambican chiefs became *regulos*, responsible for the collection of taxes, recruitment of labor, and maintenance of colonial law and order.[59] Backed by the ultimate authority of the colonial state's military capacity, the rule of the *regulos* over rural villages went largely unchallenged. But the opening of Front the Liberation of Mozambique's (FRELIMO) guerrilla war against the colonial regime in 1964—and its early successes in pushing Portuguese officials out of the rural areas of Cabo Delgado and Niassa—suddenly threw open the question of the role to be played by chiefs in the liberated zones.[60] FRELIMO, an unapologetic Marxist-Leninist party, was not inclined to see the institution of chieftaincy as an element offering a positive contribution to the building of socialism. After coming to power in 1975, FRELIMO leaders were particularly critical of any notion that the relations of traditional society were something to be respected and preserved rather than overcome and discarded. Defending the party's decision to eliminate the *regulos* and begin the difficult process of modernizing political institutions in the rural areas, a FRELIMO official stated, "The traditional feudal society is a conservative, immobile society with a rigid hierarchy. . . . It is a society which excludes youth, excludes innovation, excludes women. The correct term is gerontocracy."[61]

The chiefs did not disappear for long. By the early 1980s, the FRELIMO government was under siege by the Mozambican National Resistance (RENAMO), a counterrevolutionary movement that had been organized by the Rhodesian military in 1977, then passed on to the SADF two years later.[62] As RENAMO began to win effective control of rural territory, local-level administration of the population was returned to the former *regulos*—a reverse-image of FRELIMO's revolutionary struggle.[63] By 1990, RENAMO's successes in the field were widely attributed to their adoption of a sort of neotraditionalism: their respect for the authority of the chiefs had won them the support of the peasantry.[64] Some studies of RENAMO's rural campaign noted the extreme brutality with which villagers were often treated and argued that many communities fostered considerable hostility toward the *regulos*.[65] Nonetheless, the perception that RENAMO had reaped tremendous benefit from its alliance with traditional authority seemed to stick and was quickly adopted by the ANC leaders returning to South Africa from exile.

Jeremy Cronin, deputy secretary-general of the SACP, recalled that among ANC leaders living in exile in Mozambique, RENAMO's apparent ability to mobilize support in rural areas through the *regulos* bore an uncomfortable similarity to Inkatha's hold on rural Natal.[66] By the time the South African negotiations had begun in earnest, the notion had clearly taken hold that any attempt to eliminate the powers of chieftaincy would only cause them to return in some destabilizing new form. With the future of the entire homelands apparatus up for grabs, an NP speaker in Parliament suggested that the ANC's opposition to separate development had finally foundered on the rock of traditional authority:

> The ANC is deeply opposed to the homelands and ethnic consciousness. They have done their best to sweep away tribalism and ethnicity. Their civic organizations have been put in place to undermine traditional leaders. Self-defence units have been activated to ensure that the ANC, and not the chief, is in control. However, the ANC were told at a conference in October 1992: Do not axe the chiefs or they will come back to haunt you. The deposing of chiefs in other countries

has brought great problems. It is believed that the deposing of chiefs in Mozambique led to the formation of RENAMO and the ensuing civil war. The power of the chiefs is very real.[67]

Confirming the NP's speculations, when questioned on the ANC's plans for the chiefs under its administration, legal advisor Matthews Phosa replied, "The Mozambican Option was just one of the options we thought of, but we opted to keep the chiefs."[68] Precisely what to do with them, however, remained an open question.

5

Chiefs in the New South Africa

The early years of the 1990s seemed to represent the high-water mark of a global liberal democratic revolution. Though it was clearly not, as Francis Fukuyama famously proposed, the End of History, the collapse of old regimes and the opening of negotiations between old adversaries lent an air of inevitability to the proceedings. South Africa's own transition toward a postapartheid future began on February 2, 1990, when President F. W. de Klerk announced in Parliament that the major opposition groups—the ANC, SACP, and PAC—were to be legalized. This was to be the long-delayed step forward, in which Bantu Authorities and separate development would finally be consigned to the history books and shelved alongside colonialism and indirect rule. History, however, has been known to resist such neat cataloging and closure, and as the negotiations began for what was assumed to be a transition forward to representative democracy and the universal franchise, the doors were suddenly flung open, revealing the possibility that once set into motion, the transition could proceed in any number of different directions.

Following a year of sporadic "talks about talks," an ANC-led coalition reached agreement with the government on a framework for an all-party conference whose task would be to create the infrastructure for the eventual election of a constituent assembly: an interim government, constitutional principles and process, and a time frame for the transition. In addition to the ANC, SACP, PAC, and NP, invited parties were to include the IFP, the Azanian People's Organization (AZAPO), the Conservative Party (CP) and the Afrikaner Resistance Movement (AWB), three parties from the Indian and Colored segments of the Tricameral Parliament (a short-lived experiment in partial consociationalism), and the leaders or ruling parties of the ten Bantustan states. The list of those attending the Convention for a Democratic South Africa (CODESA) was quickly thinned by announcements that the PAC, AZAPO, the CP, and the AWB would not take part. The PAC, which had previously supported the talks, departed after becoming suspicious of a backroom deal between the ANC and the NP government. For

AZAPO, the CP, and the AWB, refusal to participate at CODESA was a simple matter of having no room for compromise.

From the IFP came a somewhat less predictable maneuver that would have far-reaching implications for the shape of the transition. As the leader of both the IFP and the KwaZulu Bantustan government, Mangosuthu Buthelezi requested the inclusion of separate delegations representing the IFP, the KwaZulu government, and the Zulu king, Goodwill Zwelithini. The arguments on behalf of the first two delegations were reasonably consistent with the negotiating forum's ground rules: the IFP requested inclusion as a political party, the KwaZulu government as a Bantustan administration.[1] But the request for a delegation to be led by the Zulu king suggested a new twist in the proceedings. Buthelezi's claim was that while the leaders of the IFP represented the interests of a political party, Zwelithini represented the institution of traditional authority and, through it, the interests of the Zulu people as a whole. Following rapidly in tow, CONTRALESA, as well as individual chiefs and several would-be kings, demanded representation at CODESA. The lid was thus lifted off the political legacy of indirect rule. For the IFP, traditional authority would become the centerpiece of its postapartheid political strategy and its campaign for constitutional autonomy in its provincial stronghold of KwaZulu-Natal. For the broader political transition South Africa was now embarking upon, the question of the role to be played by the institution of chieftaincy suddenly loomed large.

In something of a dress rehearsal for the real struggle over the future of chieftaincy (which would begin in earnest after the 1994 elections), CODESA's working groups first attempted to establish a basis on which chiefs might be permitted to participate in the talks. It immediately became clear, of course, that the way in which this question was resolved would set the tone for any political role to be played by chieftaincy in the near future. Written submissions from interested parties were requested and hearings convened for which delegations of chiefs and expert witnesses arrived to testify. CONTRALESA, allied in principle with the ANC, argued for an elected delegation of chiefs to be allowed into the negotiations. Goodwill Zwelithini's IFP-aligned spokesmen countered that the king needed his own separate delegation in order to represent properly "the specific interests of the Zulu people."[2] On the sidelines, various claimants sensed an opportunity afoot and came forward insisting that, like Zwelithini, they too were kings born of a traditional lineage and deserving of equal status and recognition.[3]

The process concluded with a delicately negotiated agreement that all chiefs (now officially renamed "traditional leaders") would be represented by a single delegation from each of the four provinces, plus five advisors.[4] What, in precise terms, their participation contributed to the final outcome of the talks is less than clear. On the one hand, the constitution that ultimately took shape from the principles laid out at CODESA included provisions accommodating and incorporating chieftaincy. On the other hand, the definition of the political space it was to fill remained vague and contradictory:

> The constitution should define a suitable role for traditional leaders consistent with the objective of a united, non-racial, non-sexist, democratic South Africa.[5]

A year later, the 1993 interim constitution offered only the most cautious of possible routes forward. Existing chiefs were to retain their positions for the time being, while provincial Houses of Traditional Leaders and a national Council of Traditional Leaders would be formed to review any legislation affecting "traditional authorities, indigenous law or such traditions and customs."[6] The question of the specific political role to be played by the chiefs would be deferred until ratification of the final constitution in 1996. The stage was thus set for a national debate sparing none of the conventional accouterments. Conferences, experts, studies, and opinion polls would all be successively wheeled out to define, defend, or attack a position on the institution of traditional authority and the proper political role to be played by traditional leaders.

Although the interim constitution had deferred the question of the political powers to be held by those designated as traditional leaders, it had quickly (and surprisingly quietly) settled the prior question of who was to be considered a traditional leader. For those who sought an answer to that question in the spate of journalistic articles and scholarly essays that rapidly appeared on the market, little could be had other than vague, quasi-anthropological definitions of chieftaincy:

> Tribal authorities are still an essential part of the political, social and economic activities of the societies in which they exist, and they symbolize political order and protection against injustice, evil and calamity. Tribal authorities may be established through inherited leadership, tribal warfare or democratic procedures. . . . The tribal leader is the most important person in the central tribal government.[7]

The political process, however, could do little with amorphous theoretical ideal-types. Thus, according to the interim constitution, any traditional authority recognized as such by the previous constitution would retain that status under the new dispensation. While identifying "the most important person in the central tribal government" might prove difficult in certain cases, locating those officially recognized as chiefs was well within the realm of the possible. The name of each and every officially recognized traditional leader in South Africa—as well as a ten-foot scroll on which his genealogy had been logged—could be found inside the filing cabinets once housed within the Native Affairs Department,[8] now transferred to the offices of the new Department of Constitutional Development. In 1994, the Department had 734 traditional leaders (those classified as chiefs, paramount chiefs, or kings) on its records.[9]

Thus, for any given rural community, traditional authority remained precisely what it had been before the transition. Just as in previous eras, the matter of succession to the chieftaincy was a swamp of ethnographic analyses and vague generalizations, laid atop an intricate reality of local-level contests, family disputes, political struggles, and a protracted history of government manipulation. Equally diverse was the real nature of the rural communities subject to traditional authority. In the middle 1980s, one researcher counted populations as small as 1,475 and as large as 37,268 under the authority of individual chiefs in Natal.[10] No standard had ever been set regarding the size of a "tribal community" and there can be no question that the political dynamics in a village of fifteen hundred and an area encompassing over thirty-five thousand would reflect dramatic and fundamental differences. Despite this, the political and legal powers of those designated as traditional leaders remained uniform; their basic outline established at the end of the nineteenth century by the Natal Code of Native Law. As local political authorities, chiefs were responsible for the maintenance of law and order, the allocation of communal land, and the administration of justice in all matters excepting crimes against the state, crimes of violence, theft, and illicit trade.

Of course, one of the more important reasons for the government's having kept such close track of its traditional leaders over the years was that it had been paying them salaries since at least the early 1950s—in many cases for much longer. The amounts received by individual chiefs varied considerably between ordinary chiefs and paramounts, between different regions, and (during the separate development era) between those who were and were not members of Bantustan legislative assemblies. In 1990, an ordinary chief might have received as little as R5,000 per year, a chief with a seat in a Bantustan legislative assembly R66,000 plus a vehicle, and King Zwelithini R305,550.[11] Not surprisingly, next in line for public debate after the question of the powers of traditional leaders was the issue of their remuneration. But far more important than the amount to be paid to the country's traditional leaders was the question of who was to pay them. Yet, in this case, the struggle was over the right, rather than the responsibility, to make out the checks. The IFP claimed the exclusive right of its KwaZulu-Natal government to pay the province's traditional leaders, while the ANC claimed the same right for the national government. In effect, both sides tacitly acknowledged the existence of a patronage regime in which chiefs occupied a middling position between the state and rural communities. As the ANC-led government of national unity proposed legislation to assume responsibility for the payment of chiefs nationwide, an IFP delegation to President Mandela led by Mangosuthu Buthelezi declared,

> Nothing could be more insulting to the autonomy of the Province and to the integrity and dignity of the Kingdom of KwaZulu than the notion of putting amaKhosi [chiefs] of our Kingdom on the payroll of the central government. This tactic has been tried before and failed. It is only because of the high regard we have for you, Mr. President, that I will not compare this type of proposal with what the English colonists attempted to do when they tried to put our amaKhosi on their payroll.[12]

In the IFP's reimagined version of South African history, the institution of chieftaincy had emerged from decades of indirect rule and apartheid effectively untouched. It remained exactly as it had been before the arrival of the first European colonist: a pure, untainted reservoir of traditional authority.

New Traditionalists

After having spent more than a decade forging his image as the Bantustan leader who refused to accept sham independence, Buthelezi instructed his IFP delegation at CODESA to withhold their endorsement of any document stating as its goal the creation of an undivided South Africa.[13] The seating of a lone IFP delegation (rather than separate contingents from the IFP, the king, and the KwaZulu government) was unjustified, Buthelezi argued, because other "ethnic nations" were represented at CODESA by the governments of their corresponding homelands.[14] After having derided the principle of ethnic representation in the 1970s, Buthelezi now seemed to accept it as fully legitimate. Indeed, the IFP now seemed to recognize the administrative apparatuses of separate development as precious and vital institutions, responsible for sustaining the spiritual essence of the Zulu nation:

> The KwaZulu Government served as an historical expression of the continuity of the Kingdom during the dark years of apartheid and its Ministers performed that function. At the present time, the Government of the Province of KwaZulu-Natal carries the historical heritage of the Kingdom of KwaZulu until the time when the Kingdom of KwaZulu is restored in terms of the April 19, 1994 Agreement by virtue of a constitution for the Province and by means of greater autonomy for the Kingdom to be achieved through international mediation.[15]

Echoing the rhetoric of Natal's nineteenth-century segregationists, the IFP warned against upsetting the delicate balance of traditional society. Any tampering with the system of traditional authority would forever alter the social landscape, ushering in that most fearsome element of modernity, the restless, angry working class. Following the end of chieftaincy, an IFP memorandum warned, "A world will have disappeared turning proud Zulus into large masses of dispossessed urban proletariat."[16]

Beginning in 1992, a series of proposed provincial constitutions were issued from the remnants of the KLA and, after 1994, from the KwaZulu-Natal provincial government, in which the IFP held a slim majority. Each contained provisions for a separate defense force, control over taxation, the ability to prevent national armed forces from entering the province, and the right to override national legislation. Their individual elements made clear enough the proposed constitutions' secessionist intent. More unique, though, was their central organizing concept: the rightful autonomy of "traditional communities." Arguments for an independent provincial military force could be easily dismissed as secessionist extremism, threatening nothing short of civil war. Claims for "indigenous rights" and the autonomy of African tradition seemed more difficult to refute.

At the center of each of the IFP's constitutional proposals lay the notion that "traditional communities" formed distinct—and rightfully autonomous—social entities. Customary law and communal land tenure were argued to represent not simply unique cultural forms, but definitive social demarcations. The duty of the state, therefore, was to defend their cultural autonomy against modern and/or Western corruption.[17] Chieftaincy, however, was argued to require a more flexible, dual role. In its central aspect, chieftaincy was the axial element of the traditional community, whose autonomy was principally secured by the standing of a traditional leader as its primary form of local government.[18] But the autonomous traditional community was not to be wholly cut off from the wider political affairs of the province. Here, too, chiefs would play the leading role. On regional councils, the second tier of the IFP's proposed system of provincial government, traditional leaders would represent their communities through a block of reserved seats. Thus, as South Africa's Human Rights Committee argued in opposition to the plan, for a political party able to secure the loyalty of the chiefs, the autonomy of traditional communities at the local level would form the foundation for provincial hegemony.[19]

The IFP's campaign to secure the autonomy of cultural communities solidified its image as the party of Zulu traditionalism. Yet, its positions were not without their contradictions in this respect. On several occasions, the demands of political expedience threatened to expose the party's traditionalist rhetoric as little more than a convenient public pose. In its haste to speed through the approval of a provincial constitution whose central tenet was the cultural autonomy of the Zulu nation, IFP officials failed to issue a Zulu translation of the document for public comment, releasing only the English-language document prepared by its American advisor, Mario Oriano-Ambrosini. And despite its stated concern for the well-being of rural black communities, the party's staunch opposition to land reform was clearly aimed at securing the support of Natal's white farming interests.[20] Far more serious, however, were the cases in which chiefs who failed to back the IFP agenda were attacked and, in one well-known case, assassinated by IFP supporters—deference to tradition ending where political contestation became sufficiently heated.[21] But, as had been the case in the internal politics of the KwaZulu Bantustan administration of the 1970s, the contradictions between political opportunism and Zulu cultural traditionalism were at their sharpest in the tortured relationship between Buthelezi and his nephew, King Zwelithini. During the run-up to the 1994 elections, the IFP had thrust Zwelithini to the front of its campaign for provincial autonomy, their refusal to participate in the elections premised on the demand for international mediators to secure a role for the king in national politics. After a series of ANC offers to guarantee his ceremonial position and salary finally convinced Zwelithini to distance himself from Buthelezi, all subsequent IFP constitutional proposals called for the king to play a strictly nonpolitical role in the "Kingdom of KwaZulu-Natal."[22]

By late 1994, then, the ANC had succeeded in pulling away what appeared to be a significant pillar of support for the IFP's traditionalist platform. But their victory in winning over a new ally in the traditional authority debate was countervailed by the slipping away of an older one. During the height of the antiapartheid struggle in the late 1980s, CONTRALESA's notion of traditional authority could be epitomized by the views of its then president, Chief Mhlabunzima Maphumulo:

> One has to move with the people. If one is leading people who are progressive I think it is right and proper to be also progressive as a leader. Because my people are MDM [Mass Democratic Movement—the alliance between the UDF and COSATU, prior to legalization of the ANC], I have to be with them. . . . CONTRALESA is aiming at the mobilization of the rural communities, so that the rural masses are in fact politicized, they know exactly what is happening, they work hand in hand with the mass democratic movement in South Africa.[23]

After Maphumulo's assassination, a radically different perspective on traditional authority began to be expounded by the organization's new president, Pathekile Holomisa:

> The institution of traditional leadership is correctly regarded by those who truly understand and cherish its role, as the repository of the norms, customs and traditions of the African people; and as the custodian of the land for and on behalf of the people. Who, then, is in a better position to articulate the direction that has to be followed under a non-racial order, on the questions of customary law and communal land, than the traditional leaders themselves?[24]

Where Maphumulo had conceived of chieftaincy as a position from which to prepare the people to lead, Holomisa understood it to be the position from which to lead the people.

Much like the IFP, upon reentering the traditional authority debate in the new postapartheid environment, CONTRALESA had begun to develop a revisionist position on the history of indirect rule and separate development. Now, rather than having fraudulently manipulated the institution of chieftaincy, the segregationist and apartheid regimes were said to have been compelled, seemingly against their will, to acknowledge and accommodate traditional authority:

> Further constitutional development took place in 1951 when the Promotion of Self-Government Act was passed by the S. A. Parliament. The Government realised the fact that it could not effect any new constitutional development without the involvement of Traditional Leaders and had no choice but to recognise them and in fact caused them to head the Territorial Authorities i.e. the Homelands. This explains why the first Chief Ministers were traditional leaders. There is no doubt that without the full participation of Traditional Leaders in the creation of the structures they would fail.[25]

CONTRALESA's call for chiefs to head all aspects of rural local government also echoed the IFP's stance.[26] But where the IFP stressed the cultural separateness and autonomy of traditional communities, CONTRALESA seemed to suggest a broadening of the powers of chieftaincy, through which traditional authority would come to apply to the country as a whole. As something "rooted in the African soil," chieftaincy's rightful destiny was to rise after the death of apartheid, rather than fall away with it. Speaking at a conference in 1994, Holomisa made the case that traditional authority was not to be understood as one cultural institution among many in a multicultural society, but as South Africa's dominant social paradigm. "CONTRALESA maintains that South Africa is a land of Kings and *Amakhosi* [chiefs]," he proclaimed, "and that accordingly, all who live in it, regardless of their race or colour, are their subjects."[27] As such, CONTRALESA now argued, traditional leaders held rightful claims to roles in all branches and at all levels of government.[28]

As much as the shift from progressive UDF ally to conservative traditionalist organization might have seemed a natural transition for chiefs concerned about their futures in the New South Africa (as one newspaper headline from early in the debate put it, "Traditional leaders may have to start looking for jobs after the elections"), it was not made without some difficulty. The assassination of chief Maphumulo in 1991 brought to the surface a factional split in CONTRALESA between the old-guard UDF activists and the new traditionalists. At the time of Maphumulo's death, Patekile Holomisa (who until then had served as CONTRALESA's vice president) assumed temporary leadership of the organization. A dispute seems then to have arisen over whether to openly support the ANC or to take a nonpartisan stance in national politics. According to CONTRALESA's former executive director, R. S. Ndou, Holomisa feared that he would not be reelected by the organization's regular national conference and organized an alternative meeting at which to ratify his leadership, packing the house with supporters—including Bantustan officials from KwaNdebele who had opposed CONTRALESA at its inception.[29] Winnie Mandela (recently fallen from the ANC's good graces for her alleged involvement in the murder of a young Soweto activist) also seems to have become involved with Holomisa's assertion of control over CONTRALESA. According to Ndou, in December 1994, Holomisa and Winnie Mandela went to Ndou's office in Johannesburg, removed the furniture, computers, telephones, and documents, and began running CONTRALESA's affairs from Winnie Mandela's private offices.[30] The character of CONTRALESA's political alliances then took something of a sharp turn. Whereas in 1989, Inkatha leaders had described CONTRALESA as, "no more than a divisive ploy to set black brother against black brother and certainly in KwaZulu to set the people against their chiefs and to set chiefs against each other," some six years later, Buthelezi and Holomisa stood together on the lawn in front of the Union Buildings in Pretoria, leading a demonstration of traditional leaders and their supporters in opposition to the ANC-led government of national unity.[31]

At the high point of the struggle over the future of traditional authority, CONTRALESA's roots as a UDF organization were virtually unrecognizable. In the Eastern Cape, home to both radical ANC-aligned activists and several of CONTRALESA's more conservative leaders, violent clashes broke out between members of the radically democratic South African National Civic Organization (SANCO) and rural chiefs.[32] As local government elections were scheduled without a clear resolution of the role to be played in them by chiefs, Holomisa announced that CONTRALESA would lead a boycott of the elections in the Eastern Cape.[33] But while some ANC leaders called for Holomisa's expulsion over his threatened electoral boycott, the party was by no means of a single mind over the question of traditional authority's place in a democratic society. From its inception, the ANC had been a broad church, encompassing a wide spectrum of political thought within its resistance to apartheid and struggle for democracy. Thus, on the question of traditional authority, rather than holding a single position with potentially contradictory elements, the ANC could be seen to harbor several sharply contradictory positions. By the middle 1990s, the dominant position was clearly that of progressive incorporation: the view that traditional authority should be accommodated within the new political structures, while gradually being shifted in a democratic direction.[34] But on either side of this middling position stood ANC members prepared to make the case for far greater, or far lesser powers to be granted to the chiefs. Against Pathekile Holomisa and Mwela Nonkonyana, both CONTRALESA chiefs and ANC members of Parliament, stood SANCO activists holding to the view (more frequently heard in the 1980s) that chieftaincy, like all other aspects of state power, required a radical democratic transformation.

The eventual dominance of the progressive incorporation paradigm, however, failed to settle the matter of the ANC's position with regard to traditional authority. For within the new structures of rural local government, traditional leaders might be incorporated in any number of different capacities: as representatives, as administrators, or as symbols of unity. Those in support of a strong political role for chieftaincy gravitated toward representation and administration as models for its rightful functions. Those who held a more critical view of chieftaincy argued that as ceremonial figures chiefs might be incorporated into local government without granting them a significant amount of political power. Throughout the debate, each of the key questions hinged on the issue of chieftaincy's legitimacy—an ironic turn of events, considering the institution's lineage. Indirect rule chieftaincy had begun its life as an ideological apparatus, designed to secure legitimacy for South Africa's colonial and segregationist states. But as the transition to nonracial democracy approached, what was once intended to legitimize the actions of higher bodies would now be examined for signs of its own independent legitimacy.

From Authority to Representation

Within the correspondence files and the annual reports of the Native Affairs Department (as well as its various renamed incarnations and offspring) considerable empirical evidence can be found to demonstrate conclusively that for many years, in many of South Africa's rural communities, men designated as chiefs played key roles in local governance. To this extent, questions strictly concerned with the powers of chieftaincy in the past could be answered decisively. The postapartheid debate over chieftaincy, however, centered on the question of which powers, if any, chiefs should continue to possess under a new constitution. This question, in turn, was connected to an assessment of the institution's legitimacy. If, in the past, the powers of chieftaincy had been derived solely from their connections to indirect rule and separate development, the claims for a continued role in government for the chiefs would have no more weight than the calls from white supremacists for the continuance of segregation. But if the powers of chieftaincy could be shown to have an autonomous base in African culture and tradition, their incorporation into the new constitution would be difficult for the leaders of a postapartheid government to reject. The debate turned, then, not on the question of power, but on the question of authority. Were chiefs simply appointed rural administrators or were they—as they now claimed to be—the bearers of *traditional authority*?

At its most basic, the notion of authority suggests a relationship between the issuer and the receiver of a statement, in which a claim is accepted or a command obeyed, not because of its contents, but because of the speaker's identity. It is in this sense that Hannah Arendt located authority as lying somewhere between coercion and persuasion, necessarily ruling out both.[35] Authority, then, indicates a hierarchical relationship whose existence is agreed upon by the parties involved in it. Arendt began her investigation of the nature of political authority in response to what she suggests as a crisis of authority in politics: the "more or less dramatic breakdown of all traditional authorities."[36] Her essay, "What is Authority?" was written in the late 1950s and although it directly addresses political developments in the advanced capitalist world, it follows a theme strikingly similar to the analyses of modernization in sub-Saharan Africa being produced contemporaneously by American and European scholars. That theme traces the roots of political crisis to a disruption of the bases of common experience and agreement. Authority, in this sense, is powerfully joined to the notion of community and suggests a relatively stable social entity endowed with clear, universal norms, as well as a corresponding (and to this extent, unique) form of hierarchy. Thus, the IFP's identification of "traditional communities as a different and specific model of societal organization" was the basis for their claim that chiefs held not only power, but rightful authority.[37]

Arendt suggests that the basis for such a collective agreement as to the nature of political hierarchy lies in the notion of a binding social foundation: the birth of a community giving rise to a precedent binding on all future generations.[38] Membership in the community commits each member to the preservation of the sacred foundation, which in turn provides for the community a form of common experience, collective agreement, and thus, legitimate authority:

> Tradition preserved the past by handing down from one generation to the next the testimony of the ancestors, who first had witnessed and created the sacred founding and then augmented it by their authority throughout the centuries. As long as this tradition was uninterrupted, authority was inviolate; and to act without authority and tradition, without accepted, time-honored standards and models, without the help of the wisdom of the founding fathers, was inconceivable.[39]

An identical claim lay at the heart of the arguments in favor of a strong political role for chieftaincy in postapartheid South Africa:

> The people of South Africa respect their leaders and likewise the Traditional Leaders have vested interest in their subjects. This is in accordance with the principle of allegiance. This bond and mutual trust existed from time immemorial and notwithstanding vicious attacks to destroy or undermine it—it exists.[40]

> *Amakhosi* . . . restate the unseverable mystical relation which makes the King of the Zulu Nation one with his Father's people, the past, present and future generations of the Zulu Nation, the sacred territory of the Kingdom and the Kingdom itself.[41]

But unseverable as that mystical bond was said to be, as KwaZulu-Natal's 1995 local government elections approached, the IFP decided that a refounding was needed. At a mass rally in a Durban soccer stadium, leaders of the organization presented a new covenant with which to bind the members of the Zulu nation, "and all the other people living in our ancestral territory to the just and noble cause of the restoration of our autonomous Kingdom."[42] Some twenty thousand people were bussed in from as far away as Johannesburg to pledge their loyalty as the covenant was read.[43] This reenactment of the founding moment could easily (and to some degree accurately) be summed up as nothing more than a preelectoral rallying of the faithful. Yet, the event was also intended to fill one of the more glaring deficiencies of traditional rule: its derivation of an active form of legitimate authority from a passive form of authorization.

Authorization stands at the center of any model of delegated authority: a consciously willed passing of power from one actor to another. The deliberate nature of the act is crucial, for it is not simply the presence of power that serves to authorize, but the consensual transfer of one person's power to another. In Roman political thought, Arendt argues, power was understood to reside in the people, while authority rested in the Senate.[44] Membership in the community and its binding tradition thus effects a transfer of power through a signification of political will. In the history of political thought, this notion of a willed authorization of hierarchy becomes all the more critical as concepts of the monarch's divine right are replaced by the individual's claim to the natural right of self-rule. Thomas Hobbes was the first to suggest a fully elaborated model of authorization in which the signification of political will contained in the authorization of a sovereign power by covenant permits the sovereign to act as though it were authorized by the independent wills of its subjects.[45] With this fictive reproduction of political will through a type of passive authorization, the words and deeds of a sovereign are understood to originate in the subjects' hearts and minds.

The fact that Hobbes's project was launched in order to explain why naturally self-ruling individuals should not be allowed to rule themselves could lead to the suspicion that there is an element in his thought of what we might now call rationalization. Though lacking the Freudian vocabulary, Rousseau suggests as much in the *Discourse on Inequality*, maintaining that the apparent absence of self-rule in civil society is better explained by force, fraud, and the compulsions of material necessity than by a fictional covenant of authorization. Much of contemporary political thought is also likely to generate friction with the Roman and Hobbesian notions of a passive authorization of power. The idea of a timeless, boundless authorization of sovereign power, enacted by a contract that is never signed and words that are never spoken does not sit well next to the democratic franchise and universal human rights. Contemporary democratic theory will prefer to root legitimate authority in the more tangible, active authorization of the ballot box.

Such methods of formal, active authorization of political hierarchy have, at certain times and in certain quarters, been identified as exclusively Western notions. It is worth remembering, though, that a considerable number of lives have been lost in the non-Western world during popular struggles to extend the democratic franchise. This is not to suggest the universality of democratic principles, but to indicate that questions of legitimate authority and political authorization cannot be settled by consulting an atlas. South Africa's twentieth-century political struggle stands as one of the clearest examples of this point, and it is for this reason that the proper political role for chieftaincy was a subject of heated public debate, rather than an element of collective common sense. At least since the disappearance of the chiefs' Upper House within the ANC in the 1940s, there could be little doubt of the fact that the central elements of popular resistance to segregation and apartheid were organized around democratic notions of authority and governance.[46] As a result, by 1990 and the long-awaited transition, even those political forces committed to the restoration of chieftaincy were forced to articulate their claims in the language of democracy. Thus, in the preamble to CONTRALESA's constitution we find hereditary chiefs bowing their heads in praise of "a democratic state based on the will of the people in a unitary, non-racial, non-sexist, free and democratic South Africa."[47]

How could a system of authority based on the idea of hereditary succession, having lost long ago any mechanisms for popular sanctions against unpopular rule, be reconciled with a "democratic state based on the will of the people?" An answer would be found in the claim that traditional authority was, in fact, an indigenous African form of democracy, different from but not inferior to Western electoral democracy. The basis for such an argument was the invocation of the historical *imbizo* or *pitso*, a communal gathering at which a chief, his council, and the community at large met to discuss the issues of the day. Through the image of the *imbizo*, traditional leaders became, for the IFP, "catalysts of consensus," more facilitators than rulers of their communities.[48] CONTRALESA's leaders adopted a similar claim:

> The seat of legislative and administrative authority in rural areas is the Great Place or Royal Place. This is where the laws governing the community are debated and enacted through discussions in open traditional gatherings, i.e. *imbizo/pitso*. The traditional leader, as head of the community, sees to the implementation of the laws through his councilors.[49]

The similarity between these images of traditional authority and the segregationist state's own pronouncements of the early 1950s is striking. In both cases, an idealized historical image has been laid over a far more complicated reality. Among studies based on contemporary fieldwork in rural Transkei and KwaZulu communities, none describes the sort of regular, consensus-based, public political process suggested by the claims for chieftaincy as a form of indigenous democracy.[50]

The search for democratic soil in which to root hereditary chieftaincy was unquestionably driven by the general climate of the postapartheid transition. In the political environment of the 1990s, "democracy" was a watchword that not even the most unapologetic supporters of the apartheid regime could afford to ignore. But for chieftaincy to square with democracy, the chiefs would have to be recognizable not only as authorities over their communities, but as representatives for their constituents. As Hanna Pitkin reminds us, despite the variety of concepts in which authority and representation are fused, they cannot be considered as identical.[51] A chief might well bind his subjects and command their obedience, but could he also be said to represent them in the political sphere? With all attention focused on questions of inclusion and the political rights of those who had previously been denied them, any case for the political powers of chieftaincy had to be capable of answering in the affirmative.

One possible route from authority to representation suggested the redeployment of chiefs as figures of symbolic unity. Much like contemporary European monarchs, South African chiefs might be transformed into living symbols of collective identity. Yet, as Michael Sutcliffe, an ANC specialist on local government in KwaZulu-Natal, noted, the notion of symbolic unity implied a strict demarcation of chieftaincy from the potentially divisive questions of politics and power:

> Now what we then said was, on the one hand, there's a need to ensure that traditional leaders and our culture, our African culture, need to be infused into local government in the way we deal with things. But secondly, we must make sure that that local government is democratic. So it was a very contradictory thing. But when we went into negotiations in Kempton Park, then we entered a bit of a battle. Because obviously traditional leaders, many of whom—probably the majority of whom—were puppets of the apartheid state, suddenly grabbed onto this and said, "No, we want to be the local government in our area, we want to be the mayor." And we said, "No, you're in fact there to be uniting the people." When you deal with local government issues, the community might have to make a decision: Do we want water or do we want sanitation? Do we want electricity this year, and where do we want that? [Traditional leaders] can't make that decision. That's a party-political decision, depending on your community, what the majority view is.[52]

As Pitkin suggests, the leader as symbol of unity becomes the object of feelings and actions, rather than an actor himself.[53] Nevertheless, the symbolic unity model was an attractive one, even for those forces committed to the ideal of a politically empowered chieftaincy. Joseph Masangu, an IFP representative for the KwaZulu-Natal House of Traditional Leaders, for example, made the case that the divisive nature of party politics necessitated the existence of symbolic chieftaincy:

> I believe, as I've said, that a rural area is a very defined area. For instance, if *amakhosi* would be elected, it would create a problem, in that they would have to be elected along political lines. I don't see a way in which they could be elected as neutral and independent persons. Should they be elected, then they must either be elected as IFP or ANC or PAC. Now that would divide their communities and it would become very difficult for an elected *inkosi* to distribute the resources in an even-handed manner. And therefore, I believe myself that the way things are . . . things must be left the way they are at the moment. Let political parties within an *inkosi*'s area compete for political power, but let an *inkosi* remain as a unifying force; a force which must in instances of dispute bring the feuding parties together and let them talk and solve their dispute.[54]

From CONTRALESA and Herbert Vilikazi, a University of Zululand sociologist called to testify at the CODESA hearings, came the suggestion that as symbols of unity, chiefs could represent politically those who did not belong to a political party.[55]

The model of symbolic unity was an attractive one to virtually all sides in the debate because of its relatively comfortable fit within the larger structures of representative democracy. Even the staunchest democrat could hardly object to a chief standing for his community as a nonpolitical symbol of unity. But for those genuinely committed to placing chiefs in positions of governance, a purely symbolic role would ultimately be unsatisfactory. Thus, after 1994 and Goodwill Zwelithini's public clashes with Buthelezi, the IFP began to advocate a strictly symbolic role for the king, but held that political and administrative powers were still necessary for the chiefs. The question that remained, however, was how hereditary authority could be included within the institutional structures of a democratic government.

The answer would be found in the politics of social identity. As Eric Hobsbawm once pointed out, although the basic questions surrounding identity politics were by no means new discoveries in the last decades of the twentieth century, the centrality of questions about social identity to politics was a distinctly novel development.[56] Much of the impetus behind modern forms of identity politics could, of course, be traced to movements in opposition to political exclusion based on forms of social identity. To this extent, the politics of social identity are often rooted in essentially universalistic principles: representative democracy and universal suffrage. Yet, it is by no means uncommon to encounter forms of identity politics in which the universalistic demand for an end to particularistic exclusion is gradually transformed into a particularistic claim to exclusive rights on the basis of identity. The first step along this path is what Pitkin refers to as a model of representation based on the correspondence of composition: the notion that a political body worthy of being called "representative" should accurately reflect the proportions and contours of the society out of which it is drawn.[57] Significant and potentially inflammatory questions are likely to remain, of course, as to the particular characteristics or identities that will be judged politically salient and deserving of inclusion.

Correspondence of composition, if it is to create or to enhance a form of representation, must assume that at some level one's political consciousness corresponds to an aspect of one's identity. A soft version of this claim might suggest that where past economic and political relations have excluded and discriminated on the basis of social identity, the road to true universalism must now run through conscious efforts to include those who were once excluded. A harder version of the connection between identity and politics, though, would seem to move in precisely the opposite direction. This would be the claim that the political affairs of a group sharing a form of social iden- tity can be managed properly only by members of that group and no other. The roots of this contention are traceable at least as far back as Montesquieu's elaboration of a theory of environmental predispositions and their corresponding forms of constitution in *The Spirit of the Laws*. Nineteenth-century theories of scientific racism took shape from similar notions of the necessary correspondence between identity and proper governance, as in Robert Knox's assertion that "every race has its form of civ- ilization."[58] In more recent times, analogous propositions have been issued in ostensibly democratic forms: localism, communitarianism, or ethnona- tional self-determination. All, however, have launched themselves from the idea of a crucial linkage between social or cultural identity and political representation.

It was precisely this nexus that would provide the framework through which calls for rural local government to be left in the hands of chiefs could be redeployed as demands entirely compatible with a modern transition to democracy. IFP leaders began to speak of a newly discovered body of "fourth generation human rights" recognizing cultural formations as entities capa- ble of assuming a mediating position between individual citizens and the state.[59] And in attendance at a 1995 United Nations conference on the rights of indigenous peoples was an organization calling itself the African Indigenous People's Council—Southern Africa Region, which included among its member organizations the IFP, the segregationist Afrikaner Volksfront, Mozambique's RENAMO, and its Angolan cousin, Jonas Savimbi's National Union for the Total Independence of Angola (UNITA).[60] CONTRALESA quickly joined the conversion to indigenism, announcing that all references to "customary law" should in the future be replaced by the term "indigenous law." Use of the word "customary," one of the organiza- tion's press releases noted, was a product of colonialism.[61]

By shifting the traditional authority debate into the register of indigenous rights, demands for the retention of an unelected system of local government could be enfolded within the broader claim—frequently championed by theories of identity politics—that a truly democratic dispensation of political rights would require unique rights to be allocated to particular cultural groups. Moving a step beyond the simple model of representation based on correspondence of composition, the claim here is that a particular group may require not only its own representatives, but its own form of representation. Thus, the advocates of traditional authority held that local government "should be developed in a manner which reflects the values of the whole community that it serves."[62] The practical definition of that community, however, could not be left to press conferences and speeches before parliamentary committees. The public face of identity politics may consist primarily of appeals to cultural difference, but the day-to-day activity of the politics of social identity is made up of ground-level organizing to demarcate a community and to keep its members inside the lines.

In this respect, the advocates of chieftaincy had been blessed with the good fortune of having inherited what otherwise would have to have been built from scratch. The physical boundaries of tribal areas had been drawn decades ago by officials of the Native Affairs Department. It now remained only for their status as separate, indigenous, traditional communities to be proclaimed and defended anew. For the isolated rural areas, this was a relatively easy case to make. But in its push toward the grand vision of separate development, the NP government had defined several segregated townships adjacent to major urban centers as tribal areas and placed them under the authority of chiefs. With the transition to nonracial democracy, such communities were generally expected to be reincorporated into the greater metropolitan areas they adjoined. But as the supporters of empowered chieftaincy began to assert a radical form of indigenist identity politics, it became clear that the reincorporation of the periurban townships was by no means a fait accompli.

Just as the transition-era struggle between the ANC and IFP had been especially sharp and protracted in KwaZulu-Natal, with a low-level civil war continuing to smolder through the middle 1990s, the debate over the demarcation of urban and rural communities in the Durban metropolitan area was also particularly heated. There, a board of experts was appointed to study the contested areas and make recommendations regarding their relationship to the metropolitan electoral districts. In the majority of cases, the demarcation board identified strong functional linkages between the periurban areas and metropolitan Durban. Had a normal process of development occurred, there would have been no question as to their unity. Only the fictions of apartheid had allowed them to remain administratively separate.[63] Chiefs in the periurban areas, however, were lobbied by the IFP to resist incorporation, and several who had initially favored it quickly reversed their positions.[64] A panel of jurists convened to decide the issue appeared to have been swayed by the stack of identical letters from chiefs demanding that their areas be kept separate from Durban, and the apartheid-era boundaries between urban and tribal areas were allowed to stand.

The existence of such boundaries was vital for the claim that hereditary chieftaincy deserved to be accommodated within the larger framework of representative democracy. Yet, a close examination of the demarcation between the traditional community and the modern society revealed a highly permeable barrier, if any at all. One could select from a wealth of different aspects of daily life and fail to find any whose elements were wholly circumscribed by the village, the chief, and tribal tradition. Economic surveys conducted in rural KwaZulu in the early 1980s, for example, showed that over ninety percent of rural household incomes included some form of wage labor in the formal economy.[65] Reflecting a perfect translation of traditional authority into market economic hierarchy, the same study revealed that many of KwaZulu's *izinduna* (a chief's appointed lieutenants) were also small business owners.[66] Although the system of communal land tenure and the allocation of land by chiefs were frequently put forward as the centerpiece of traditional social organization, South Africa's rural landscape was by now a patchwork of different land tenure systems. Many rural villages under communal tenure sat across a road or only a few kilometers away from plots under individual tenure, administered by Christian missions. Gradual incursions of the market economy had also transformed land tenure practices. Markets for ostensibly communal land had been known to exist for years.[67]

As for the chiefs themselves, despite having now been designated as "traditional leaders," anyone serving in the institution of chieftaincy since at least the early 1900s had been deeply and inextricably tied to the modern state and economy. Graham Callanan's 1986 study of the day-to-day tasks of a KwaZulu chief, for example, recorded in diary form such entries as:

08.15   Salesman arrived from Pietermaritzburg with a car which he asked the chief to test drive. (The chief is at present looking for a small automatic car for his wife.)

09.00   To magistrate's office at the local town to pay one of his accounts, which is in arrears. Showed receipt to magistrate and the case against him was withdrawn.

09.45   Returned to Makhathini to collect a salary cheque and deposited this at the local bank in town. Spoke to bank manager concerning his slight overdraft which has now been rectified.

11.00   Informed by the Town Clerk's secretary that the head of the town's protection services wished to see him.[68]

It could, perhaps, be suggested that chieftaincy functioned as a conduit between the worlds of tradition and modernity, but by 1990 and the transition to nonracial democracy, this too became increasingly implausible. Even in the highly unlikely event that apartheid-era political events had entirely passed by some of those in the rural areas, the onset of the transition and the end of the racialized franchise now meant that even those in the most distant villages would not only have a stake in national electoral politics, their support would be actively canvassed by national political parties.

One further example of the permeable nature of cultural boundaries between tradition and modernity lay within the controversy surrounding the carrying of so-called traditional weapons. In early 1990, as the violent clashes between IFP and ANC supporters began to spread nationwide, IFP leaders encouraged their followers to arm themselves with spears, knives, clubs, and shields. When ANC leaders called for a ban on the carrying of such weapons at public demonstrations, Buthelezi responded that cultural tradition required all Zulu men to do so. To ban the carrying of traditional weapons, he declared, would amount to a form of cultural genocide:

> Cultural weapons . . . are a tool of self-identification as a minority, and a reminder of their ethnic roots and history. Taking away the cultural weapons means depriving the Zulus of their chosen and traditional tools of self-identification. It is a strategy to destroy the Zulu ethnic identity and awareness, and to intimidate them in the most militant expression of their identity. It is a well planned form of cultural castration which is meant to be received both as an intimidation and a provocation.[69]

The feared cultural castration, however, had already taken place more than sixty years prior. The carrying of "assegais, knives, kerries, sticks or other weapons or instruments by Natives" had been prohibited in the Union of South Africa in 1923.[70] A ban on the carrying of traditional weapons was also written into the legal codes of the KwaZulu Bantustan and was actively enforced by the chiefs.[71] It was only a presidential proclamation, quietly issued by F. W. de Klerk in 1990, that had legalized the carrying of weapons "in accordance with traditional Zulu usages, customs or religions."[72] Having paved a legal path for the carrying of traditional weapons, the apartheid state then began manufacturing spears for the IFP.[73] Somewhat more potent G3 assault rifles were also supplied to KwaZulu chiefs, and in an ironic (albeit deadly) twist, marchers at a Durban protest against the Government of National Unity's 1996 ban on traditional weapons used several of these rifles to fire on police, trying to disarm them.[74]

The tangled threads interweaving culture, identity, economic relations, and politics should come as no surprise to us. A study based on life-history interviews with Zulu-speakers in KwaZulu-Natal, for example, revealed the existence of multiple forms of identity, spliced fragments of tradition and modernity, and few clear connections between cultural identity and political belief.[75] When asked to describe his Zulu culture, one respondent linked it to ceremonies such as traditional dancing at weddings. He went on to explain, however, that there had been no dancing at his own wedding because, "since we are now Christians we have forbidden those customs, as we now proceed along Christian lines."[76] The fragmentation of identity is a hallmark of modernity, yet the possibility for multiple interpretations of the connection between identity and action is not necessarily limited to cosmopolitan urbanites. In 1955, a meeting of chiefs in northern Natal called to discuss the proposed Promotion of Bantu Self-Government Act concluded with the following resolution:

> That the translation of the Bantu Act makes no clear meaning in Zulu. "Zibuse" refers: Rule Yourself. Does it mean as an individual, or as a group? If as a group, which group?[77]

Reification of the Mask

If the existence of discrete tribal social formations was the first critical element of the case for chieftaincy's inclusion within South Africa's new non-racial democracy, its necessary complement was the legitimacy of chiefly authority within such communities. Apart from a few notable exceptions,[78] a pronouncement of that legitimacy opened nearly every commentary on contemporary chieftaincy produced during the transition years:

> Before considering the position of traditional leaders and their structures, it is necessary to make the point that their continued existence is beyond doubt. To suggest their demise is shortsighted and foolish. They enjoy the support and respect of a large majority of their subjects and provide a unifying and stabilizing function in society.[79]

> However, the historical specificity of the South African socio-economic landscape is that there has been a juxtaposition of the modern mode of production with the traditional one. This has resulted in a society characterised in the main by two value systems, modern and traditional. The majority of the people in the countryside still owe allegiance to chiefs and it was for this reason that even the apartheid regime used them for their own purposes.[80]

> It may be safely accepted that chiefs still enjoy substantial support in rural areas and play a significant role in the lives of tribespersons.[81]

As for evidence of chieftaincy's legitimacy, little was offered, apart from the argument that the institution's continued existence was, in itself, a demonstration of its legitimate status. CONTRALESA's leader, for example, held that the legitimacy of chieftaincy could be seen in the fact that whereas the urban structures of apartheid had been eliminated during the transition, in the rural areas, the chiefs had remained in power.[82] Alastair McIntosh offered the readers of academic journals a more scholarly version of the same claim:

If the notion that chiefs are "all powerful" is swept away, the question is raised as to how chiefs continue to obtain legitimacy. The idea that the institution of chieftainship is viewed as wholly illegitimate is difficult to sustain. Dlamini's surveys (1987) suggest that the tribal court is preferred to the magistrates' courts amongst respondents throughout KwaZulu districts. This is echoed by Marais (1989) whose survey amongst 54 chiefs revealed that 10 percent of chiefs had never had cases being taken on appeal to the magistrate.[83]

Here, the external signs of authority are offered as proof of its internal workings. Command and compliance are taken as indications of common experience and collective agreement. What is lacking is any sign of the specific nexus between a belief in the legitimacy of chiefly authority and an act of compliance. We are presented with only the final part of the equation.

Compliance, however, might be traceable to any number of different origins other than the legitimate authority of a chief. An apparent preference on the part of rural villagers for the chief's court rather than that of the magistrate could be explained by familiarity, convenience, or the existence of a language barrier. In the 1980s and 1990s, education levels remained extremely low in South Africa's rural areas, and the knowledge that bringing a case to the magistrate would have required a Zulu, Xhosa, or Sotho-speaker to deal in English or Afrikaans could easily have deterred villagers from leaving the familiar structures of the chief's authority. The tenuous conditions of existence for most rural households left them highly susceptible to stronger forms of compulsion, as well. Income levels for rural households remained very low in the last quarter of the twentieth century, and while the power of a chief to dispossess someone of their land was said to be used only rarely, it nonetheless existed.[84] A family's loss of residence rights in a rural village would have meant both the loss of land used to grow subsistence crops and likely exile to the squalid conditions of a periurban squatter camp.

Such conditions produced fertile ground for the development of patronage practices by chiefs and indunas. A 1984 study of 320 rural households in randomly selected districts in KwaZulu reported that nearly ninety percent had been required to make some form of payment to a chief or an induna in return for the allocation of "communal" land. Many were also forced to keep up an annual payment in order to be allowed to plant.[85] Similar systems of payment for land allocation were reported in studies of the Transkei.[86] Irregular taxation or "tribute" was commonly collected by chiefs for the purchase of a car, a new house, or a son's marriage.[87] Some forty percent of those surveyed in the 1984 KwaZulu study described it as a common practice to pay a chief or induna before applying for pensions or disability grants from the state.[88] Many of these payments amounted to relatively small amounts, but as Paulus Zulu argues,

While in relative terms . . . even a sum of R5 is insignificant, by the standards of the rural aged, widows and disabled, these are perceptibly substantial figures. Add to this the stated long delays, harassment and the alleged indifference from clerical officials, and one has a perfect recipe for passivity and apathy.[89]

As one respondent in a study of the Transkei suggested, patronage might also provide a perfect recipe for silent compliance: "No applicant can be so stupid as to expose [patronage] when he has actually got the land which he desperately wanted."[90] During the postapartheid transition years, chiefs continued to assert control over the allocation of land within the territories previously demarcated as tribal areas. Although no data similar to that obtained by Zulu was collected during the 1990s, a survey conducted in 1995 found that only twenty-one percent of rural residents seeking land felt that chiefs should be solely responsible for the allocation of land. Thirty-eight percent felt that chiefs should share responsibilities for land allocation with government officials, while forty-one percent felt that chiefs should have no role in the allocation of land.[91]

Patronage provided one powerful foundation for the powers of chieftaincy, but the most obvious source of their support was the one most frequently overlooked by researchers, journalists, and pundits: the inscription of chiefly authority in the law. In one respect, Zulu's study of chieftaincy in KwaZulu supports McIntosh's assertions as to the popular preference for bringing legal matters to the chief rather than to a higher official in the modern state apparatus. Of Zulu's 320 respondents, seventy-six percent stated that the chief or an induna was the person to whom they would most likely bring a problem.[92] But unlike the studies cited by McIntosh, Zulu went on to ask a significantly more revealing question: the respondent's reasons for doing so. The majority of those giving an answer replied, "It's a regulation that we go to him."[93] And indeed it was. The judicial powers of chieftaincy had been defined and underpinned by the modern state since 1891 in Natal, and since 1927 in the whole of South Africa. In some instances, respect for chieftaincy was itself prescribed by law.[94]

Patronage, coercion, legal compulsion, or cultural tradition might result in outwardly indistinguishable acts of compliance. Graham Callanan seems to have realized as much while observing the daily life of a KwaZulu chief, and his study concludes on a distinctly unsettled note:

> The true feelings that people have of Chief Gumede are, moreover, difficult, if not impossible to determine on the basis of observation alone, for even those critical of his actions show outward respect. . . . For these various reasons much of the discussion which follows is rather superficial.[95]

Observation may fail to discern between apparently identical forms of behavior produced by sharply divergent dynamics. Yet, the origins of compliance

are critical to our understanding of its nature. Consider the perfect counterfeit note. It would be identical in all of its directly observable features to
genuine currency. Its status as a clever forgery rather than a piece of legal
tender is determined not by its appearance, but by its point of origin:
Treasury Department or basement printing press. Yet, its origins are invisible
as we hold the bill in our fingers. The perfect counterfeit would be shrouded
in an illusion produced by the mystification of its history.

What confronts us in the case of chieftaincy's legitimacy, then, is the possibility of an illusion generated by the institution's detachment in time and
space from its origins. An analogous problem lies at the heart of Marx's concept of commodity fetishism:

> The mysterious character of the commodity-form consists therefore simply in the
> fact that the commodity reflects the social characteristics of men's own labour as
> objective characteristics of the products of labour themselves, as the socio-natural
> properties of these things. . . . It is nothing but the definite social relation between
> men themselves which assumes here, for them, the fantastic form of a relation
> between things. In order, therefore to find an analogy we must take flight into the
> misty realm of religion. There the products of the human brain appear as
> autonomous figures endowed with a life of their own, which enter into relations
> both with each other and with the human race. So it is in the world of commodi-
> ties with the products of men's hands. I call this the fetishism which attaches itself
> to the products of labour as soon as they are produced as commodities, and is
> therefore inseparable from the production of commodities.[96]

Value is granted to commodities by their position within a set of human relationships. Yet, the separation of commodities in time and space from their
direct producers creates the illusion of their autonomous possession of
value. The true nature of the commodity form can only be understood by
examining its social origins. As commodities themselves appear to us in daily
life, however, their connections to the process of production disappear; only
their status as objects of exchange remains.

Slavoj Zizek suggests that, like Freud's analysis of the dream, Marx's examination of the commodity form is intended not simply to reveal the hidden
content within a formal exterior, but to explain the secret of the form itself.[97]
For Freud, the latent desire or wish is concealed within the manifest form of
the dream-text. Yet, the dream's secret is not so much its encoded message as
the process of its encoding. The dream, for Freud, is a way of thinking under
the peculiar conditions of the physical state of sleep.[98] As we wake and
recount the manifest content of the dream, it becomes a frozen text, seemingly disconnected from the process that has produced it. It is this detachment of the dream-text from its origins that masks the dream's true meaning.

An analogous process occurs through the embodiment of beliefs in material institutions and practices. Zizek offers an example of this phenomenon in his interpretation of the Tibetan prayer wheel. In the Tibetan Buddhist ceremony, a prayer is written on a piece of paper, the paper is inserted into a wheel, and the wheel is turned. Thus, whatever the true nature of the participants' thoughts, objectively they are praying; objectively they believe.[99] The problem is brought into especially sharp relief in an example suggested by Hanna Pitkin. Punishment, Pitkin argues, denotes the harm done to a person who has broken a law or violated a norm. To refer to a harmful act as a type of punishment, then, is to legitimize it. Crucially, though, the distinction between punishment and harm—between a legitimate and an illegitimate act—is drawn by the disposition of the action's object: convicted criminal or innocent victim. The harm done to someone who has broken a law is not harm, but punishment. Likewise, the harm done to someone innocent of any crime could not be considered punishment; it remains simply harm. But with the establishment of formal institutions through which punishment is to be meted out, it becomes possible for harm done to innocent persons to appear as punishment. Regardless of the factual histories surrounding each prisoner in a state penitentiary, as they stand in the prison yard, wearing their prison uniforms, they appear as though they are being punished.[100] Some may, in fact, be experiencing punishment; others may be experiencing harm. But detached from the circumstances of their conviction and sentencing, those being harmed become indistinguishable from those being punished. The danger of reification is that in the place of an institution whose task it is to perform legitimate acts, we may find before us an institution whose acts appear legitimate, no matter what their actual content.

In a footnote to *Capital* vol. I, Marx hints at the possibility of a similar dynamic taking hold in the political sphere:

> Determinations of reflection of this kind are altogether very curious. For instance, one man is king only because other men stand in relation as subjects to him. They, on the other hand, imagine that they are subjects because he is king.[101]

Here, too, is an illusion generated by the detachment of an object or phenomenon from its origins. As the subjects gaze up at their monarch, his power appears as an independent property of his being. In reality, uncoupled from the willingness of the subjects to recognize his authority, the king's power vanishes. Yet, it is precisely the illusory independence of the king's position that works to legitimize his rule. The fact that the king is king becomes a reason to obey his commands. Coercion or patronage might, at any particular moment, provide the true impetus behind a subject's obedience to a king's authority, but detached from its origins, that obedience lodges neatly within the ideology of monarchy, supporting the image of the king as rightful recipient of the subject's deference. It is exactly this sort of ideological illusion that anthropologist John Comaroff reveals in his explanation of an apparent paradox within the process of chiefly succession in southern African Tswana communities. Despite clear cultural traditions dictating a single line of hereditary succession, Tswana chieftaincies are routinely beset by numerous competing claims to the throne. Upon closer examination, Comaroff argues, the ascendancy of any particular chief can be revealed to depend upon multiple sources of political power. Having defeated his rivals, however, the successful claimant assumes the mantle of cultural tradition, implying that he had been the sole legitimate successor all along.[102]

The contradictions surrounding the institution of chieftaincy, then, cannot be resolved other than through a recognition of its function as an ideological apparatus. We cannot know, in other words, whether or not chieftaincy is legitimate, because a central element of the institution's purpose is the production of the appearance of its own legitimacy. Over the gritty realities of coercion and patronage, chieftaincy drapes the veil of communal tradition. Just as with the reinvention of chieftaincy by indirect rule, we find here a specular mechanism, intended to produce a fused image of hierarchy and identity for those to be interpellated as tribal subjects. But an additional aspect of chieftaincy's functioning as an ideological apparatus now also becomes clear: the image of chieftaincy's legitimacy is produced by its reification of consent. Here, as in all institutions of hereditary rule, the dynamic human activity of consenting to authority is frozen in the body of an institutional object. The potentially uneven and variable quality of the act of consent is transformed into the neat, uniform substance of cultural identity. The membership of subjects in their tribal community presumes their authorization of whoever emerges as chief through the process of succession—or whoever appears to emerge from such a process. It is precisely because the act of authorization has been reified by the institution of hereditary rule that its particular form of legitimate authority can be counterfeited with comparative ease.[103]

* * *

In 1966, D. H. Reader's ethnographic survey, *Zulu Tribe in Transition,* described the "remarkable" survival of the institution of chieftaincy in the social life of rural Zulu-speakers.[104] By that year, the Bantu Authorities Act had been in effect for well over a decade and the construction of the homelands system was already seven years underway. Both policies would have been nearly unimaginable had the institution of chieftaincy not been continuously maintained and controlled by the colonial and segregationist states for more than a century. Was the survival of chieftaincy any more remarkable than, say, the survival of a national police force? Reader's mistake was to see in chieftaincy a mystical, rather than a mundane form of power. His error is not one that has been eliminated by the passage of time. In 1994, the ANC's deputy minister for Provincial Affairs and Constitutional Development, Vali Moosa, ended his introduction of the Council of Traditional Leaders Bill to Parliament saying,

> In conclusion, for as long as the people who live in faraway valleys, majestic green hills, on widely stretched out plains and mountainsides honour and support traditional leaders, the Government of the day will support and respect traditional leaders, as they are the custodians of people's culture and we are a people's government.[105]

In truth, for as long as the state supports and sustains the institution of hereditary rule, the presumption of its legitimacy will fall naturally into place. It is worth noting, though, that any similar form of authorization by racial, ethnic, or other forms of social identity will be subject to the same vulnerability. We may be tempted to believe that all of those who share a form of ascribed identity have through their assumption of that identity preauthorized both hierarchy and leadership within their ranks. Such assumptions are likely to conceal far more complex realities and open the way for counterfeiting operations undertaken by both state institutions and aspiring political entrepreneurs.

Epilogue

Constitutions often speak loudest in their silences, the most difficult and contentious issues frequently being set aside by constitutional architects for future generations to resolve. The political role of chieftaincy stood as just such an issue for South Africa's 1996 constitution. An entire section of the document was devoted to the subject of "Traditional Leaders," yet that section comprised only fifteen lines of text. Echoing the CODESA negotiations and the 1993 interim agreement, the 1996 constitution officially recognized traditional leadership, but offered no specific guidance as to the powers or roles of traditional leaders.[1] The chiefs continued to preside over land allocation and customary law in rural communities. The state continued to pay their salaries.

The institution of chieftaincy also remained a flash point for political tension. As the country's 2000 municipal elections approached, a loose coalition of chiefs threatened to disrupt the balloting in rural areas unless their demands for political power were met. The announcement of a date for the elections was pushed back as government officials negotiated with chiefs linked to both the IFP and CONTRALESA. The local elections eventually went ahead, with the chiefs receiving a promise from the ANC government that they would be granted a form of guaranteed representation on local councils.[2]

In September 2003, a white paper on traditional leadership finally emerged from the Department of Provincial and Local Government.[3] The white paper represented a significant step forward in the legal definition of a role for chieftaincy. The eighty-page document examined, in substantial detail, the history and institutional structure of South African chieftaincy, before making recommendations for a revised framework in which it might now function. Three months later, a bill based on the white paper's recommendations was adopted by Parliament. The 2003 Traditional Leadership and Governance Framework Amendment Act centered on a dual definition of traditional leadership, suggesting that both cultural tradition and legal recognition would demarcate the roles of traditional leaders. Like the interim constitution, the act declared that all those previously recognized by the South African state as traditional leaders would retain their legal status as such.[4] Future succession processes would be directly overseen by royal families (defined as the immediate relatives of the ruling family within a traditional community), with government officials certifying the status of the successor.[5] The roles to be played by traditional leaders were similarly split between cultural and governmental functions. Traditional leaders were charged with responsibility for "functions provided for in terms of customary law and customs of the traditional community concerned," though the act also provided considerable latitude for future legislation permitting traditional leaders to play active roles in land administration, justice, economic development, environmental management, and tourism.[6]

To this extent, the 2003 Act largely mirrored earlier pieces of legislation regulating the institutions of chieftaincy, suggesting both a vaguely defined sphere of customary authority and a more specific range of tasks to be delegated to chiefs by government officials. Yet, the 2003 Act also announced significant modifications designed to reconcile the undemocratic and patriarchal aspects of traditional authority with postapartheid South Africa's progressive political spirit. Officially recognized "traditional communities" would be required to establish "traditional councils" to assist and guide traditional leaders in their work. Traditional leaders would nominate sixty percent of the councils' membership; the remaining forty percent would be popularly elected. Women would be required to make up at least one-third of the membership of each traditional council.[7] The legislation also provided for a certain amount of government oversight of traditional leadership. A national Commission on Traditional Leadership Disputes and Claims would now investigate and seek to resolve questions involving the demarcation of traditional communities or the succession of traditional leaders. Finally, a code of conduct for traditional leaders—requiring transparency, efficiency, and the promotion of unity—was attached to the new law.

The ANC's aims in establishing traditional councils with elected membership and guaranteed positions for women were clear enough in the context of the organization's historical development. Since its adoption of the Freedom Charter in 1955, the ANC had committed itself to the proposition that "South Africa belongs to all who live in it, black and white."[8] From that point forward, ANC leaders strongly asserted the social and political irrelevance of race against the racial nationalism of the rival PAC, whose leaders maintained that South Africa rightfully belonged to those of African ancestry exclusively.[9] The ANC's progressive orientation was then further deepened during its years in exile. After its exile from South Africa in the early 1960s, the ANC became entirely dependent for its survival on support from foreign governments and solidarity organizations. Nelson Mandela's 1962 tour of newly independent African countries won promises of assistance, though the leaders of those states possessed little ability to deliver. The decolonized countries were economically weak and those sharing a border with South Africa had little capacity to resist any military pressure the apartheid state might have chosen to apply. As a result, the bulk of support for the exiled ANC came from the Soviet Union, East Germany, and the Scandinavian social democracies. The effect on the ANC's ideological valence was profound. The organization increasingly associated itself with "the world's progressive forces" and looked toward the building of "a non-racial, ultimately non-national world society; a society without class."[10] Thus, in all of its most crucial aspects, the institution of chieftaincy collided head-on with the progressive, modernist agenda advanced by most ANC leaders of the exile generation. Rather than the modernist vision of legal equality, chieftaincy suggested both hereditary and patriarchal privilege. Instead of the nonracialist ideal of a society in which categories of race or ethnicity would cease to function as institutionalized political divisions, traditional authority suggested the continued assignment of political membership on the basis of ascribed identity. Traditional leaders, then, might be accommodated, but their practices would also have to be transformed substantially in order to correspond with the party's goals of legal and political equality.

By the late 1990s, however, a sea change was underway within ANC circles. As the collapse of the Soviet Union weakened ANC connections to international socialism, the organization's ascension to governing power in postapartheid South Africa boosted the confidence of African nationalists who now began to reclaim the ideological ground once ceded to the PAC. Leading the turn was Thabo Mbeki. Mbeki's father, Govan, had been a leading member of the South African Communist Party, and in the early 1970s, Thabo had studied at the Lenin School in Moscow.[11] Yet, as he assumed the post of deputy president in 1994 (rising to state president in 1999), Mbeki began to espouse both capitalism and African nationalism. His stirring speech, "I am an African" (delivered at the signing of the 1996 constitution), was suffused with African traditionalist imagery, while his policy framework as state president was organized around his vision of an African Renaissance. The claims of the chiefs—who since CODESA had rooted their concept of traditional authority in the imagery of African ethnoracial identity—found newly sympathetic ears in Mbeki's increasingly dominant wing of the party. For those ANC leaders now asserting a reinvigorated version of African cultural pride, the arguments in favor of traditional authority were irresistible.

By 2003, the contradictory pressures impelling ANC leaders toward both progressive and traditionalist agendas produced a correspondingly contradictory approach to the institution of chieftaincy. Both the white paper on traditional leadership and the 2003 Traditional Leadership Act depicted chieftaincy as an institution rooted in the cultural traditions of rural communities and (during the colonial, segregationist, and apartheid eras) unjustly manipulated by outsiders.[12] Yet, both documents concluded with recommendations for the modification of chieftaincy's powers, roles, supporting institutions, and succession rules.[13] On the one hand, then, chieftaincy was portrayed as being worthy of respect and preservation because of its status as the unique product of precolonial African tradition. On the other hand, chieftaincy was simultaneously and unproblematically represented as something thoroughly malleable—capable of being refashioned and turned to any purpose set for it by government.

A similar set of tensions pervaded the government's approach to the question of land rights. Some of the most important—and most brutal—aspects of racial segregation in South Africa had centered on access to land. As a result, the postapartheid transition necessarily involved the question of how land rights might be restored to individuals, families, or communities who had been forcibly removed during the drives to partition the country along racial lines. A land claims commission was established to investigate cases of forced removals and by 2003, more than 36,000 claims (involving some 83,000 households and 500,000 hectares of land) had been settled.[14] Although there was no separate accounting of their numbers, many chiefs were reported to have filed claims for tribal lands confiscated during the apartheid era.[15] In one case, Douglas Zondo, chief of the Empangisweni community in northern KwaZulu-Natal, won control of seven thousand hectares of prime agricultural land worth more than two million dollars.[16]

Yet, the restitution process represented only one aspect of the complicated struggle the ANC now faced in its attempts to transform land rights in the wake of apartheid. Millions of people continued to live in rural areas under forms of land tenure secured only by customary law. On the one hand, government officials sought to give formal legal standing to the land rights of those still living in the former Bantustans and segregated reserves. On the other hand, the chiefs were unlikely to accept quietly a reformation of rural land rights that failed to grant them substantial authority in the allocation process. Land was one of the key material foundations on which the powers of chieftaincy rested. "Without communal land," declared Mpiyezintombi Mzimela, chairman of the National House of Traditional Leaders (NHTL), "there is no traditional leadership."[17] Once again, debates raged between community activists concerned that chiefs would be granted too much power and chiefs worried that they would receive too little.[18]

The legislation that finally emerged provided for land held under forms of communal tenure to be registered to communities, with individuals receiving deeds of communal land rights.[19] Land administration committees would be established in rural communities to allocate and oversee communal land. Where a traditional council existed (as defined by the Traditional Leadership Act), it would function as the land administration committee.[20] But having granted chiefs considerable leverage over land allocation and management, the new law also included one important check on their power. Dispossessions of land would have to be ratified by a land rights board, consisting of government appointees, representatives from each Provincial House of Traditional Leaders, representatives of industry, and members of the affected community.[21] Not long after passage of the Communal Land Rights Act, challenges to it were filed with the Constitutional Court by community and legal rights activists charging that it would have the effect of further entrenching the autocratic powers granted to chiefs under indirect rule.[22] At the time of this writing, the cases remained open.

In the first decade after the passage of South Africa's postapartheid constitution, the most troubling issues surrounding the institution of chieftaincy continued to linger. In anticipation of the 2004 national and provincial elections, political violence flared in rural KwaZulu-Natal districts under the jurisdiction of IFP-affiliated chiefs.[23] As the 2006 municipal elections approached, Mangosuthu Buthelezi once again invoked his self-declared status as "traditional prime minister" to call a mass-meeting of the Zulu Kingdom in Durban.[24] Like the 1995 meeting called under similar circumstances, the *imbizo* was intended to cement Zulu ethnic identity and the traditional authority of the chiefs to electoral support for the IFP. Deputy President Jacob Zuma was chosen, because of his ability to speak as an ethnic insider, to issue an ANC call to boycott the exercise. The morning after some seven thousand people attended the event, Zuma commented, "I am a Zulu. You didn't see me at the *imbizo*."[25] Yet, despite Zuma's statements aimed at decoupling ethnic identity from partisan politics, the government's reservation of special rights and powers for tribal chiefs did little to erode the IFP's ability to use the chiefs as a political machine in rural areas.

The accommodation of chieftaincy also seemed to leave in place the possibility for patronage networks to be reestablished between government departments, the chiefs, and their subjects. In 2004, Deputy President Zuma announced the opening of new facilities for chiefs in Mpumalanga, including a traditional court and king's chamber, built at a cost of R5 million.[26] In the Eastern Cape, it was revealed that provincial officials had purchased eight BMW X5s for high-ranking chiefs and the chairman of the provincial House of Traditional Leaders when two of the vehicles were damaged in road accidents.[27] Such luxurious facilities and vehicles could only serve to increase the perceived gap in status between chiefs and their subjects, as well as invite the funneling of largesse to constituents inclined toward compliance.

But now that the chiefs had secured positions in government, to what ends were those positions being put? When I conducted interviews with chiefs in KwaZulu during the 1990s, I routinely asked them about their policy agendas: "If you were given positions of power in rural local government, what changes or goals would you pursue?" The answers I received were equally routine: "Chiefs must be in control of rural areas." The men I spoke to were adamant that chiefs be granted the powers of government, but had nothing to say with respect to their reasons for seeking such powers. By contrast, the National House of Traditional Leaders has been both more visible and more politically dynamic than the individual chiefs themselves. After a wave of deaths during Xhosa circumcision ceremonies, the NHTL appointed a task team to investigate.[28] At a national conference of traditional leaders, called by the NHTL in December 2005, the agenda focused on four key issues: opposition to same-sex marriages (which the conference deemed a "wicked, decadent and immoral Western practice"), discouraging the commercialization of *lobola*, support for cooperative government and capacity-building, and the establishment of a Continental House of Traditional Leaders.[29] Three conclusions might be drawn from this list. First, the chiefs had begun to stake out for themselves a conservative position with respect to cultural issues. Second, the representatives elected to the NHTL appeared at least nominally willing to cooperate with the ANC government's vision of power-sharing in rural governance and development. Third, the chiefs could be expected to pursue any new opportunities that might arise to increase the scope of their power.

The roles envisioned for chiefs by the ANC could not be more different from those imposed by the segregationist and apartheid governments. Chiefs would now be expected to participate in economic development and the pursuit of gender equality, rather than the political repression of rural communities. But the question might still be posed: If economic development and gender equality were desirable goals, why grant even partial responsibility for their achievement to a hereditary office? Surely elected local councils with mandated representation for women could assist in coordinating rural development efforts as well as traditional leaders and their partially appointed, partially elected traditional councils. But the postapartheid sanctification of chieftaincy had little to do with administrative capacity. Instead, it was driven by the belief that an African government would be remiss in failing to recognize and entrust with political power figures revered within African cultural tradition. As in all types of racial, ethnic, and religious reification, there is here a type of Sartrean bad faith: the assumption that culture plots for us an inescapable destiny, when, in truth, our choices to accept, reject, or modify cultural practices are our own.

There was also within the ANC's approach to chieftaincy a certain resonance with the legacy of indirect rule. For the colonial, segregationist, and apartheid governments, the choice to preserve and reproduce the external form of chieftaincy while modifying its contents was motivated by the belief that chiefs possessed a unique cultural connection to African subjects: Africans might sneer at the mine foreman or try to dodge the police officer, but place one of their own chiefs in front of them and they would be bound by their very nature to obey his commands. Though its aims were unquestionably different, the ANC's attempt to retain the trappings of traditional authority while modifying its political function was, in this sense, identical to the ideological strategy of indirect rule. To the extent that its future efforts succeed in promoting social development and access to political rights, the ANC's approach to rural governance will represent a long delayed step forward. Yet, the reservation of special rights and powers assigned on the basis of cultural tradition fails to confront the potentially repressive face of cultural identity. The instant legitimacy conferred upon an institution or practice by its designation as "traditional" short-circuits the processes of dialogue, debate, and participatory decisionmaking that lie at the heart of democracy.

Notes

Preface

1. Gail M. Gerhart, *Black Power in South Africa: The Evolution of an Ideology* (Berkeley: University of California Press, 1978), 237.

2. Tom Lodge, *Black Politics in South Africa Since 1945* (Johannesburg: Ravan Press, 1983), 210.

3. Robert M. Price, *The Apartheid State in Crisis* (New York: Oxford University Press, 1991), 21.

4. Louis Althusser, "Ideology and Ideological State Apparatuses," in *Lenin and Philosophy* (New York: Monthly Review Press, 1971).

Chapter 1

1. United Kingdom Colonial Office, *Summer Conference on African Administration, Eighth Session* (London: H. M. Stationary Office, 1957), 81.

2. Mahmood Mamdani, *Citizen and Subject: Contemporary Africa and the Legacy of Late Colonialism* (Princeton: Princeton University Press, 1996).

3. Mamdani, *Citizen and Subject*, 37.

4. See, for example, A. Adu Boahen, *Africa Under Colonial Domination, 1880–1935* (Paris: UNESCO, 1990), 143.

5. Mamdani, *Citizen and Subject*, 39.

6. For example, the Kikuyu, Kamba, and Masai societies of Kenya, and the Ibo of Nigeria maintained councils of elders and men of ability "whose positions depended on tendering good advice and having it accepted by their peers," but they had no single figures who corresponded to the position of an authoritarian or hereditary chief. Robert Tignor, "Colonial Chiefs in Chiefless Societies," *Journal of Modern African Studies* 9, no. 3 (1971): 341.

7. United Kingdom Colonial Office, *Summer Conference on African Administration, Eighth Session*, 13.

8. See, for example, Norman Etherington, "The 'Shepstone System' in the Colony of Natal and Beyond the Borders," in *Natal and Zululand from Earliest Times to 1910*, ed. Andrew Duminy and Bill Guest (Pietermaritzburg: University of Natal Press, 1989), 172.

9. Edgar Brookes, *The History of Native Policy in South Africa* (Pretoria: J. L. Van Schaik, 1927), 30.

10. Ibid.

11. Jeff Guy, *The Destruction of the Zulu Kingdom* (Pietermaritzburg: University of Natal Press, 1994), 69–70.

12. Jeff Guy, "The Destruction and Reconstruction of Zulu Society," in *Industrialization and Social Change in South Africa*, ed. Shula Marks and Richard Rathbone (New York: Longman, 1982), 175.

13. John Lambert, "Chiefship in Early Colonial Natal," *Journal of Southern African Studies* 21, no. 2 (1995): 279.

14. "[The capitalist state's] fundamental distinctive feature seems to be the fact that it contains no determination of subjects (fixed in this state as 'individuals,' 'citizens,' 'political persons') as *agents of production*; and that this was not the case in other types of state." Nicos Poulantzas, *Political Power & Social Classes* (London: Verso, 1978), 123 (emphasis in original).

15. Guy, "The Destruction and Reconstruction of Zulu Society," 181.

16. See, for example, Howard Rogers, *Native Administration in the Union of South Africa* (Johannesburg: University of the Witwatersrand Press, 1933), 124.

17. On precolonial land allocation in Natal and Zululand see King Cetshwayo's evidence to the Cape Commission on Native Laws and Customs, reprinted in *A Zulu King Speaks*, ed. C. de B. Webb and J. B. Wright (Pietermaritzburg: University of Natal Press, 1987), 88. For practices in the Cape see Colin Bundy, *The Rise & Fall of the South African Peasantry* (Cape Town: David Philip, 1988), 18–21.

18. Mamdani, *Citizen and Subject*, 138.

19. Jean-Jacques Rousseau, "Discourse on the Origins of Inequality," in *The Basic Political Writings*, trans. and ed. Donald. A. Cress (Indianapolis: Hackett, 1987), 58–59.

20. Thomas Pakenham, *The Scramble for Africa* (New York: Random House, 1991), 600.

21. Niccolo Machiavelli, *The Prince*, trans. George Bull (London: Penguin Books, 1999), 54.

22. Ibid., 30–31.

23. Ibid., 36.

24. Max Weber, "Politics as a Vocation," in *From Max Weber: Essays in Sociology*, ed. H. H. Gerth and C. Wright Mills (New York: Oxford University Press, 1946), 78.

25. Max Weber, *The Theory of Social and Economic Organization* (New York: Free Press, 1957), 382.

26. Machiavelli, *The Prince*, 39. Former CIA officer John Stockwell offered a strikingly similar assessment in his account of the agency's involvement in the Angolan civil war: "Possibly you don't understand about mercenaries. Their code is money and their only loyalty is to money. There aren't half a dozen in the world who can be paid in advance and still fulfill their contracts when it's hot and dirty and the rockets start landing on the battlefield. With mercenaries you pay as they perform, not before." John Stockwell, *In Search of Enemies* (New York: W. W. Norton & Company, 1978), 221.

27. Machiavelli, *The Prince*, 68.

28. Weber, "Politics as a Vocation," 78–79.

29. Ibid.

30. Louis Althusser, "Ideology and Ideological State Apparatuses," 127–28.

31. Karl Marx, "Preface to *A Contribution to the Critique of Political Economy,*" in *The Marx-Engels Reader,* ed. Robert C. Tucker (New York: Norton, 1978), 4–5.

32. G. A. Cohen, *Karl Marx's Theory of History: A Defence* (Princeton: Princeton University Press, 1978), 134.

33. Karl Marx and Friedrich Engels, "Manifesto of the Communist Party," in *Later Political Writings,* ed. Terrell Carver (Cambridge: Cambridge University Press, 1996), 1–2.

34. George C. Comninel, *Rethinking the French Revolution* (New York: Verso, 1987), 166–67.

35. Cohen, *Karl Marx's Theory of History,* 150.

36. Althusser, "Ideology and Ideological State Apparatuses," 132–33.

37. Compare the highly specific assignment of roles within a feudal society ("You are to till this piece of land, for this member of the nobility, forever") to the far more abstract rules of a capitalist order ("You are to maximize your individual well-being, in any way that you can, provided the rules of private property are respected").

38. Despite the fact that Marx's 1859 preface is usually cited as a source of the technological determinist model of historical materialism, it also seems to contain support for a model in which historical outcomes are understood to be the result of contingent class struggles fought (at least in part) with ideological weapons: "In considering such transformations a distinction should always be made between the material transformation of the economic conditions of production, which can be determined with the precision of natural science, and the legal, political, religious, aesthetic or philosophic—in short, ideological forms in which men become conscious of this conflict and fight it out." Marx, "Preface to *A Contribution to the Critique of Political Economy,*" 5.

39. Althusser, "Ideology and Ideological State Apparatuses," 169.

40. Ibid., 143.

41. Ibid., 144–45.

42. Ibid., 157.

43. Ibid., 161, 170.

44. Terry Eagleton, *Ideology* (New York: Verso, 1991), 142.

45. Althusser, "Ideology and Ideological State Apparatuses," 162.

46. Ibid., 180 (emphasis in original).

47. Ibid., 174.

48. Brookes, *The History of Native Policy in South Africa,* 49–50.

49. Natal Ordinance 3 of 1849, quoted in T. W. Bennett, *A Sourcebook of African Customary Law for Southern Africa* (Cape Town: Juta & Co., 1991), 113.

50. Mamdani, *Citizen and Subject,* 115; Bennett, *A Sourcebook of African Customary Law for Southern Africa,* 129.

51. Brookes, *The History of Native Policy in South Africa,* 175.

52. S. D. Girvin, "Race and Race Classification," in *Race and the Law in South Africa,* ed. A. Rycroft (Cape Town: Juta & Co., 1987), 4.

53. It should be noted that Althusser's thesis suggests only a difference in emphasis between the RSA and the ISAs. The RSA is said to function *mainly* through violence; the ISAs *mainly* through ideology. However, this does not rule out (and

Althusser specifically suggests the inclusion of) elements of coercion in the operation of the ISAs and ideological functions within the RSA. Althusser, "Ideology and Ideological State Apparatuses," 145–46.

54. John Cell, *The Highest Stage of White Supremacy* (Cambridge: Cambridge University Press, 1982), 49. Botha's position was supported in the findings of a 1903 study by the Transvaal Labour Commission. See Adam Ashforth, *The Politics of Official Discourse* (Oxford: Oxford University Press, 1990), 24–25.

55. Quoted in Saul Dubow, *Racial Segregation and the Origins of Apartheid* (London: Macmillan Press, 1989), 23.

56. Shula Marks, *The Ambiguities of Dependence in South Africa* (Johannesburg: Ravan Press, 1986), 132n18.

57. Marks, *The Ambiguities of Dependence in South Africa*, 40. In 1937 a similar defense of segregation was written by Nicholls for the South African Native Affairs Department. See Union of South Africa Native Affairs Department (NAD) correspondence files, 1950, 260, 278, National Archives, Pretoria, South Africa.

58. A. R. Radcliffe-Brown, "Some Problems of Bantu Sociology," *Bantu Studies* 1 (1921–22), 38.

59. Rogers, *Native Administration in the Union of South Africa*, 250; NAD, *Annual Report, 1922–26* (Pretoria: Union of South Africa Government Printing Office, 1926), 1.

60. Brookes, *The History of Native Policy in South Africa*, 501.

Chapter 2

1. Union of South Africa, Act 38 of 1927, sec. 31; 35.

2. Ibid., sec. 1; Natal Code of Native Law, reproduced in Rogers, *Native Administration in the Union of South Africa*, 316.

3. NAD, *Annual Report, 1935–36* (Pretoria: Union of South Africa Government Printing Office, 1936), 14.

4. Ibid.; NAD, *Annual Report, 1944–45* (Pretoria: Union of South Africa Government Printing Office, 1945), 5; NAD, *Annual Report, 1945–47* (Pretoria: Union of South Africa Government Printing Office, 1947), 4.

5. Isaac Schapera, ed., *The Bantu-Speaking Tribes of South Africa* (London: Routledge, 1937); N. J. Van Warmelo, *A Preliminary Survey of the Bantu Tribes of South Africa* (Pretoria: Union of South Africa Government Printing Office, 1935).

6. In some cases, different candidates for succession might be backed by separate factions in the population. In 1946, one such case arose in a village near Rustenburg. Four different men (each with an element of popular support) claimed the right to the local chieftaincy. Acting as state ethnologist, Van Warmelo selected the winning candidate, declaring him to be "the only possible person." See NAD correspondence files, vol. 322, 26/55, National Archives, Pretoria, South Africa. In other cases, candidates for succession were supported by the local population but rejected by the state. See, for example, NAD correspondence files, vol. 12, 29/1, National Archives, Pretoria, South Africa.

7. Union of South Africa, Government Notice 2252 of 1928, sec. 7.

8. Ibid., sec. 13.

9. J. M. Mohapeloa, *Africans and Their Chiefs* (Cape Town: African Bookman, 1945), 4; William Beinart, *The Political Economy of Pondoland, 1860 to 1930*

(Johannesburg: Ravan Press, 1982), 15–17, 22; Bundy, *The Rise & Fall of the South African Peasantry*, 16.

10. Althusser, "Ideology and Ideological State Apparatuses," 180.

11. [J. B. Peires], "Ethnicity and Pseudo-Ethnicity in the Ciskei," in *The Creation of Tribalism in Southern Africa*, ed. Leroy Vail (Berkeley: University of California Press, 1989), 396.

12. Govan Mbeki, *The Peasants' Revolt* (London: International Defence and Aid Fund for Southern Africa, 1984), 34.

13. Rogers, *Native Administration in the Union of South Africa*, 57.

14. Mbeki, *The Peasants' Revolt*, 36.

15. Union of South Africa: Act 12 of 1936.

16. Marian Lacey, *Working for Boroko* (Johannesburg: Ravan Press, 1981), 64.

17. Mirjana Roth, "Elections under the Representation of Natives Act," in *Resistance and Ideology in Settler Societies*, ed. Tom Lodge (Johannesburg: Ravan Press, 1986), 160–61.

18. NAD correspondence files, vol. 13, 37/1, National Archives, Pretoria, South Africa.

19. Ashforth, *The Politics of Official Discourse*, 121.

20. Ibid., 122, 134.

21. Rex Reynolds, *Searchlight on South Africa's Native Policy* (Pretoria: Union of South Africa State Information Office, 1947).

22. Ibid., 6, 8.

23. See Deborah Posel, "The Meaning of Apartheid before 1948," *Journal of Southern African Studies* 14 (1987).

24. For example, Minister of Native Affairs E. G. Jansen's claim: "This side of the House says that they can have their rights in their own area but not in the European area." Union of South Africa, *House of Assembly Debates*, 7 September 1948, col. 1727.

25. NAD, *Annual Report, 1945–7*, 29–30.

26. Department of Bantu Administration and Development, *Annual Report, 1951–2* (Pretoria: Union of South Africa Government Printing Office, 1952), 7.

27. Union of South Africa, *House of Assembly Debates*, 7 September 1948, col. 1730.

28. Quoted in Ashforth, *The Politics of Official Discourse*, 76.

29. Brian Lapping, *Apartheid: A History* (New York: George Braziller, 1987), 131.

30. See for example E. Hudson, J. J. Van Tonder, J. F. Eloff, J. B. De Vaal, and R. E. Lighton, *Race Studies for Standard VII* (Cape Town: Nasionale Boekhandel Beperk, [undated publication]).

31. NAD, *Annual Report, 1935–6*, 1; NAD, *Annual Report, 1949–50* (Pretoria: Union of South Africa Government Printing Office, 1950), 43.

32. Union of South Africa: Act 68 of 1951; Govt. Notice no. 939, 8 May 1953.

33. Quoted in Gwendolen M. Carter, Thomas Karis, and Newell M. Stultz, *South Africa's Transkei* (Evanston: Northwestern University Press, 1967), 48–49.

34. Quoted in Mbeki, *The Peasants' Revolt*, 57.

35. Department of Bantu Administration and Development, *Annual Report, 1954–57* (Pretoria: Union of South Africa Government Printing Office, 1957), 52.

36. For example, David Hammond-Tooke, an anthropologist for the Native Affairs Department from 1954 to 1958, was asked to assist in "finding" chiefs for the

Mfengu—a difficult task given that any recognizable form of Mfengu chieftaincy had vanished over a century earlier. See Carter et al., *South Africa's Transkei*, 50.

37. David Hammond-Tooke, *Command or Consensus* (Cape Town: David Philip, 1975), 209.

38. John L. Comaroff, "Chiefship in a South African Homeland," *Journal of Southern African Studies* 1, no. 1 (1974), 42.

39. NAD correspondence files, vol. 8993, 214/362, National Archives, Pretoria, South Africa.

40. NAD correspondence files, vol. 8931, 232/362, National Archives, Pretoria, South Africa; Sec. 5 of the 1927 act provided for the definition of tribal and location boundaries, the fusion and fission of tribes, and the removal of tribes and individuals.

41. J. A. S. Nel, quoted in Carter et al., *South Africa's Transkei*, 49.

42. Department of Bantu Administration and Development, *Annual Report, 1954–7*, 49.

43. Sec. 2 of the 1951 act provided for consultation with the communities concerned prior to the establishment of a tribal authority.

44. NAD correspondence files, vol. 8993, 214/362, National Archives, Pretoria, South Africa.

45. Department of Bantu Administration and Development, *Annual Report, 1952–3* (Pretoria: Union of South Africa Government Printing Office, 1953), 5.

46. NAD correspondence files, vol. 8993, 214/362, National Archives, Pretoria, South Africa.

47. Union of South Africa, Government Notice no. 2252, 21 December 1928.

48. Mbeki, *The Peasants' Revolt*, 105.

49. A memo from the chief Native commissioner for the Western areas to the secretary in Pretoria reads: "Every effort is at present being made to obtain and in other cases, retain the confidence of the natives. The assistance of native chiefs is being sought in the Department's betterment and rehabilitation schemes and they are being called upon to do more and more work for and on behalf of the Department. I feel that, if increments however small cannot be granted in all cases, the Department should consider allowing them to continue drawing the salaries they receive at present." NAD correspondence files, vol. 12, 26/1, National Archives, Pretoria, South Africa.

50. Colin Bundy, "Land and Liberation," in *The Politics of Race, Class and Nationalism in 20th Century South Africa*, ed. Shula Marks and Stanley Trapido (London: Longman, 1987), 268.

51. Mbeki, *The Peasants' Revolt*, 98–99.

52. NAD correspondence files, vol. 7665, 40/332, National Archives, Pretoria, South Africa.

53. Ibid.

54. NAD correspondence files, vol. 20, 61/1, National Archives, Pretoria, South Africa.

55. Hammond-Tooke, *Command or Consensus*, 105–7.

56. NAD correspondence files, vol. 12, 29/1, National Archives, Pretoria, South Africa.

57. Ibid.

58. Bundy, "Land and Liberation," 274; I. B. Tabata, *The All African Convention: The Awakening of a People* (Johannesburg: People's Press, 1950).

59. NAD correspondence files, vol. 12, 29/1, National Archives, Pretoria, South Africa.

60. Bundy, "Land and Liberation," 279, q.v., E. P. Thompson, "Eighteenth-Century English Society: Class Struggle without Class?" *Social History* 3, no. 2 (1978), 154. William Beinart suggests similarly that "Bantu Authorities were opposed because they seemed to deliver chiefs into the hands of the government rather than because they involved chiefs." William Beinart, "Chieftaincy and the Concept of Articulation," in *Segregation and Apartheid in Twentieth-Century South Africa*, ed. William Beinart and Saul Dubow (London: Routledge, 1995), 185.

61. Mbeki, *The Peasants' Revolt*, 114–15; Tom Lodge, *Black Politics in South Africa since 1945* (Johannesburg: Ravan Press, 1983), 280; Roger Southall, *South Africa's Transkei* (New York: Monthly Review Press, 1983), 110; NAD correspondence files, vol. 20, 61/1, National Archives, Pretoria, South Africa; NAD correspondence files, vol. 7695, 485/332, National Archives, Pretoria, South Africa.

62. Mbeki, *The Peasants' Revolt*, 113; NAD correspondence files, vol. 284, 279/53, National Archives, Pretoria, South Africa.

63. NAD correspondence files, vol. 7665, 40/332, National Archives, Pretoria, South Africa.

64. All ideological apparatuses, then, are not ideological *state* apparatuses. Both the Kongo's attempt at its own manipulation of the institution of chieftaincy and its allegiance to the All African Convention indicate the presence of ideological apparatuses not only separate from the state, but in competition with it for the right to interpellate subjects.

65. African National Congress, *The Powers of the Supreme Chief* (Johannesburg: R. L. Esson & Co. Ltd., 1928).

66. Ibid., 3.

67. Ibid., 2.

68. Anton Lembede, "National Unity Among African Tribes," *Inkundla ya Bantu*, 2nd Fortnight, October 1945, quoted in Gail M. Gerhart, *Black Power in South Africa*, 61.

69. Gerhart, *Black Power in South Africa*, 148.

70. Ibid., 68.

71. Quoted in Ashforth, *The Politics of Official Discourse*, 76.

72. Quoted in Jeffrey Butler, Robert I. Rotberg, and John Adams, *The Black Homelands of South Africa* (Berkeley: University of California Press, 1977), 25.

73. State Department of Information, *Multi-National Development in South Africa: The Reality* (Pretoria: Republic of South Africa Government Printing Office, 1974), 26.

74. Union of South Africa, Act 46 of 1959.

75. Quoted in Rob Davies, Sipho Dlamini, and Dan O' Meara, *The Struggle For South Africa* (London: Zed Books, 1985), 204–5.

76. *New York Times*, 1 March 1954; State Department of Information, *Multi-National Development in South Africa: The Reality*, 20–23.

77. Republic of South Africa, Act 48 of 1963.

78. See, for example, Carter, Karis, and Stultz, *South Africa's Transkei*; Butler, Rotberg, and Adams, *The Black Homelands of South Africa*; Southall, *South Africa's Transkei*.

79. Quoted in Gerry Mare, *African Population Relocation in South Africa* (Johannesburg: SA Institute of Race Relations, 1980), 75.

80. Butler et al., *The Black Homelands of South Africa*, 126.

81. Ibid., 4; Newell M. Stultz, "Some Implications of African 'Homelands' in South Africa," in *The Apartheid Regime*, ed. Robert M. Price and Carl G. Rosberg (Berkeley: Institute of International Studies, 1980), 214.

82. Southall, *South Africa's Transkei*, 16–17.

83. [Jeff Peires], "Ethnicity and Pseudo-Ethnicity in the Ciskei," 397.

84. Julia Segar, *Fruits of Apartheid* (Bellville: Anthropos Publishers, 1989), 86.

85. NAD, *Annual Report, 1949–50*, i.

86. Minister of Native Affairs E. G. Louw, quoted in Aletta J. Norval, *Deconstructing Apartheid Discourse* (New York: Verso, 1996), 158.

87. Republic of South Africa, Act 79 of 1961.

88. Department of Bantu Administration and Development, *Annual Report, 1960–62* (Pretoria: Republic of South Africa Government Printing Office, 1962), 10–11.

89. Department of Bantu Administration and Development, *Annual Report, 1965* (Pretoria: Republic of South Africa Government Printing Office, 1965), 12.

90. Archie Mafeje, "An African Chief Visits Town," *Journal of Local Administration Overseas* 2, no. 2 (1963).

91. David Welsh, "The Growth of Towns," in *The Oxford History of South Africa*, vol. 2, ed. Monica Wilson and Leonard Thompson (London: Oxford University Press, 1971), 231.

92. Muriel Horrell, *Legislation and Race Relations* (Johannesburg: South African Institute of Race Relations, 1971), 43; Marie Wentzel, "Historical Origins of Hostels in South Africa: Migrant Labour and Compounds," in *Communities in Isolation: Perspectives on Hostels in South Africa*, ed. Anthony Minnaar (Pretoria: Human Sciences Research Council, 1993), 5.

93. David Coplan, "The Emergence of an African Working-Class Culture," in *Industrialization and Social Change in South Africa*, ed. Shula Marks and Richard Rathbone (London: Longman, 1982), 360.

94. Martin Legassick, "Legislation, Ideology and Economy in Post-1948 South Africa," *Journal of Southern African Studies* 1, no. 1 (1974), 16.

95. Robert M. Price, *The Apartheid State in Crisis* (New York: Oxford University Press, 1991), 130–31.

96. Ibid., 133.

97. South African Communication Service, *This is South Africa* (Pretoria: Republic of South Africa Government Printing Office, 1993), 26.

98. Price, *The Apartheid State in Crisis*, 193–95.

Chapter 3

1. Antonio Gramsci, *Selections from the Prison Notebooks*, trans. and ed. Quentin Hoare and Geoffrey Nowell Smith (New York: International Publishers, 1971), 57.

2. Alan Brooks and Jeremy Brickhill, *Whirlwind Before the Storm* (London: International Defence and Aid Fund for Southern Africa, 1980), 207–8, 212.

3. *Rand Daily Mail,* 25 August 1976.

4. Gavin Woods, "Hostel Residents—A Socio-Psychological and Humanistic Perspective," in *Communities in Isolation: Perspectives on Hostels in South Africa,* ed. Anthony Minnaar (Pretoria: Human Sciences Research Council, 1993), 69–70.

5. Wentzel, "Historical Origins of Hostels in South Africa: Migrant Labour and Compounds," 6.

6. Brooks and Brickhill, *Whirlwind Before the Storm,* 321.

7. *Star,* 24 August 1976.

8. *Rand Daily Mail,* 25 August 1976; *Star,* 24 August 1976.

9. "Iphi iBlack Power? Sifikile thina Inkatha kaZulu [Where is Black Power? We of Inkatha kaZulu are here]," *Rand Daily Mail,* 26 August 1976; Brooks and Brickhill, *Whirlwind Before the Storm,* 217.

10. *Star,* 27 August 1976; *Rand Daily Mail,* 27 August 1976.

11. Brooks and Brickhill, *Whirlwind Before the Storm,* 219–20; Thula was later called to the Protea Police Station by Minister of Police Jimmy Kruger and told not to interfere with the events at Mzimhlope. *Rand Daily Mail,* 27 August 1976.

12. Brooks and Brickhill, *Whirlwind Before the Storm,* 218.

13. Ibid., 212.

14. *Rand Daily Mail,* 23 August 1976.

15. Brooks and Brickhill, *Whirlwind Before the Storm,* 213.

16. *Star,* 25 August 1976.

17. *Rand Daily Mail,* 25 August 1976.

18. Ibid.

19. *Rand Daily Mail,* 26 August 1976.

20. Ibid.; in 1976, homes in Soweto would have been the property of the West Rand Administration Board, rented, but not owned by residents.

21. *Star,* 26 August 1976.

22. Ibid.

23. *Star,* 25 August 1976.

24. After meetings between SSRC leaders, Gibson Thula, and men from the hostel, a third strike was carried off successfully with the support of the Mzimhlope workers. Brooks and Brickhill, *Whirlwind Before the Storm,* 230.

25. Johan L. Olivier, "Political Conflict in South Africa: A Resource Mobilization Approach," in *Capturing the Event: Conflict Trends in the Natal Region 1986–1992,* ed. Simon Bekker (Durban: University of Natal Centre for Social and Development Studies, 1992), 1. The figure quoted here is drawn from the records of the South African police.

26. *New York Times,* 20 August 1990.

27. Hermann Giliomee, "Explaining the Slaughter," *Star,* 24 August 1990; Donald L. Horowitz, "The Beginning of the End," *New Republic,* 26 November 1990; Donald L. Horowitz, *A Democratic South Africa?* (Berkeley: University of California Press, 1991); Anthony Minnaar, *Conflict and Violence in Natal/Kwazulu* (Pretoria: Human Sciences Research Council, 1991).

28. See John Aitchison, "The Civil War in Natal," in *South African Review* 5, ed. G. Moss and I. Obery (Johannesburg: Ravan Press, 1989); Michael Sutcliffe and Paul Wellings, "Inkatha Versus the Rest," *African Affairs* 87, no. 348 (1988); Anthony Minnaar, "Undisputed Kings: Warlordism in Natal," in *Patterns of Violence,* ed. Anthony Minnaar (Pretoria: Human Sciences Research Council, 1992).

29. Olivier, "Political Conflict in South Africa."

30. Rupert Taylor, "The Myth of Ethnic Division: Township Conflict on the Reef," *Race and Class* 33, no. 2 (1991), 5.

31. One assault on a Johannesburg commuter train involved several groups making coordinated attacks as the train passed through different stations—a textbook "bloody nose" ambush. *Weekly Mail*, 28 June 1991. See, for example, James W. McCoy, *Secrets of the Viet Cong* (New York: Hippocrene Books, 1992), 255.

32. *New York Times*, 14 December 1990.

33. *New York Times*, 12 June 1991.

34. *New York Times*, 20 July 1991; *Weekly Mail*, 19 July 1991; *Weekly Mail* 2 August 1991.

35. Department of Defence, *White Paper on Defence and Armament Production* (Pretoria: Republic of South Africa Government Printing Office, 1977), 3.

36. Fourteen areas were identified as targets for state strategic planning: intelligence, security, military, political, economic, psychological, scientific/technological, religious/cultural, manpower services, national supplies, resources and production, transport and distribution, financial services, community services, and telecommunication. Robert M. Price, *The Apartheid State in Crisis* (New York: Oxford University Press, 1991), 86.

37. Helmoed-Romer Heitman, "Some Possibilities in Counter-Insurgency Operations," quoted in African National Congress, *Statement to the Truth and Reconciliation Commission*, August 1996, sec. 4.7, African National Congress Archives, Johannesburg, South Africa. See also *Weekly Mail*, 24 November 1989; *New York Times*, 22 October 1996.

38. "The counter-revolutionary troops and militiaa . . . must realize that their ultimate objective is not just to destroy the revolutionary forces, but to mobilize the population in support of the governing power. . . . Friendship and respect are the only bases by which the military can gain the co-operation and intelligence that it requires for its operations." John J. McCuen, *The Art of Counter-Revolutionary War* (Harrisburg: Stackpole Books, 1966), 60–62.

39. Quoted in *Weekly Mail*, 20 May 1988. Compare with McCuen's text: "Thus it is, that the final step in mobilizing the masses is counter-revolutionary organization of the people. This organization must be accomplished in great depth. . . . This organization will require the governing authorities to foster all sorts of classes, associations, clubs, groups, and societies. They may be designed for social, vocational, sports, agricultural, educational, medical, religious, military, or other suitable activities. . . . They will make the population receptive to persuasion." McCuen, *The Art of Counter-Revolutionary War*, 58.

40. Steven Mufson, *Fighting Years: Black Resistance and the Struggle for a New South Africa* (Boston: Beacon Press, 1990), 275.

41. "The second distinguishing characteristic is the institution of a *public force* which is no longer immediately identical with the people's own organization of themselves as an armed power. This special public force is needed because a self-acting armed organization of the people has become impossible since their cleavage into classes." Frederick Engels, *The Origin of the Family, Private Property, and the State* (New York: International Publishers, 1968), 229–30 (emphasis in original).

42. *Cape Times*, 12 July 1996.

43. Nicholas Haysom, *Mabangalala* (Johannesburg: University of the Witwatersrand Centre for Applied Legal Studies, 1986), 22.

44. Ibid., 110.

45. *Weekly Mail*, 30 May 1986.

46. *Weekly Mail*, 27 June 1986.

47. *Weekly Mail*, 21 February 1992.

48. *Weekly Mail*, 3 January 1992; *Weekly Mail*, 17 January 1992; *Weekly Mail*, 31 January 1992.

49. See Lourens du Plessis, "Covert Operations: Front Companies," in *The Hidden Hand: Covert Operations in South Africa*, ed. Anthony Minnaar, Ian Liebenberg, and Charl Schutte (Pretoria: Human Sciences Research Council, 1994).

50. Maqina later admitted to receiving funds from AEC, but denied knowledge of its links to the government. *Weekly Mail*, 10 January 1992. On Ama-Afrika's assaults on UDF supporters, see Catholic Institute for International Relations, *Now Everyone is Afraid* (London: Catholic Institute for International Relations, 1988), 91–99.

51. Du Plessis, "Covert Operations: Front Companies," 238.

52. Holomisa took command of the Transkei in a coup on 30 December 1987. After taking power, his sympathies for the antiapartheid movement began to be revealed. In 1992, he released documents to the press detailing the government's covert actions against antiapartheid activists. For background on the Transkeian coup, see J. B. Peires, "The Implosion of Transkei and Ciskei," *African Affairs* 91 (1992).

53. Transkei Office of the Military Council, *How the South African Government Manipulates and Destabilizes Black Communities* (press release distributed at Port Elizabeth Holiday Inn: 11 March 1993, document in the author's collection), 2–3. References to the Katzen documents can also be found in Rich Mkhondo, *Reporting South Africa* (London: James Currey, 1993), 75.

54. On machinations in Ciskei, see Peires, "Implosion of Transkei and Ciskei," and [Peires], "Ethnicity and Pseudo-Ethnicity in Ciskei."

55. Transkei Office of the Military Council, *How the South African Government Manipulates and Destabilizes Black Communities*, 7–8, 13, 21.

56. Peires, "Implosion of Transkei and Ciskei," 368.

57. In 1987 a similar attempt was made to establish an ethnopolitical organization in Venda known as the Thari ya Sechaba Cultural and Liberation Movement. Recruits were given military training and shown anti-ANC films, but it too apparently met with little success. *Weekly Mail*, 15 May 1987.

58. Critical studies of the organization include Roger Southall, "Buthelezi, Inkatha and the Politics of Compromise," *African Affairs* 80, no. 321 (1981); Gerhard Mare & Georgina Hamilton, *An Appetite for Power: Buthelezi's Inkatha and the Politics of Loyal Resistance* (Johannesburg: Ravan Press, 1987); Mzala, *Gatsha Buthelezi: Chief with a Double Agenda* (London: Zed Books, 1988). Supportive studies include Lawrence Schlemmer, "The Stirring Giant: Observations on the Inkatha and Other Black Political Movements in South Africa," in *The Apartheid Regime: Political Power and Racial Domination*, ed. Robert M. Price & Carl G. Rosberg (Berkeley: Institute of International Studies, 1980); John Kane-Berman, "Inkatha: The Paradox of South African Politics," *Optima* 30 (1982); John D. Brewer, "The Membership of Inkatha in Kwamashu," *African Affairs* 84, no. 334 (1985). A particularly interesting attempt at

explaining the relationship between Buthelezi and the South African state (albeit mainly by historical analogy) is found in Shula Marks, *The Ambiguities of Dependence in South Africa* (Johannesburg: Ravan Press, 1986).

59. Mare and Hamilton, *An Appetite for Power*, 55.

60. *Weekly Mail*, 2 August 1991.

61. Mzala, *Gatsha Buthelezi*, 91.

62. Compare with Heitman's description of misinformation operations: "The intelligence services can also create some havoc by the supplying of false information, particularly the type to create mistrust. Thus a leader of the insurgency could be made to appear as a police-informer by, for instance, paying him more or less secretly, or, less subtly by rewarding him publicly." African National Congress, *Statement to the Truth and Reconciliation Commission*, sec. 4.7.

63. *Weekly Mail*, 8 December 1995.

64. Patrick Lekota, interview by author, Bloomfontein, South Africa, 4 April 1996.

65. The first large-scale attack was made by Inkatha forces on demonstrators in Umlazi and KwaMashu protesting the assassination of UDF activist Victoria Mxenge in August 1985. Inkatha was credited by local officials and the mainstream English press with having restored order to Durban. See Haysom, *Mabangalala*, 86–91.

66. Lekota, interview by author.

67. *Weekly Mail*, 25 March 1988.

68. *Weekly Mail*, 10 January 1992.

69. Magnus Malan, several other SADF officers, and M. Z. Khumalo were charged in November 1995 by the KwaZulu-Natal attorney general with responsibility for the 1987 KwaMakutha massacre in which thirteen people were killed when Inkatha members, allegedly trained and deployed by the SADF, attacked the home of Victor Ntuli. All those charged were acquitted in October 1996. The judge in the case, Justice Jan Hugo, argued that although the prosecution had proven that Inkatha forces were armed and trained by the SADF, they failed to prove a sufficiently direct link between the accused and the specific incident of murder in the indictment. See *Sunday Independent*, 21 April 1996; *Sunday Tribune*, 21 April 1996; *Daily News*, 22 April 1996.

70. *Sunday Independent*, 21 April 1996.

71. Ibid.

72. Ibid.

73. *Mail & Guardian*, 3 May 1996.

74. *Mail & Guardian*, 8 December 1995.

75. *Cape Times*, 21 September 1996.

76. Jeremy Baskin, *Striking Back: A History of COSATU* (London: Verso, 1991), 72.

77. UWUSA's leadership included President P. S. Ndlovu (personnel manager for Tongaat-Hulett Sugar), General Secretary S. Z. Conco (director of Khulani Holdings—an Inkatha investment group), Vice President P. Msomi (a township superintendent), Treasurer P. Davidson (director of Kuhlani Insurance Brokers—also Inkatha-owned). Mare and Hamilton, *An Appetite for Power*, 132.

78. *Weekly Mail*, 26 July 1991.

79. Ivor Powell, "Aspects of Propaganda Operations," in *The Hidden Hand: Covert Operations in South Africa*, ed. Anthony Minnaar, Ian Liebenberg, and Charl Schutte (Pretoria: Human Sciences Research Council, 1994), 338.

80. Former security policeman Paul Erasmus provided information on the SSC's post-1990 operations after leaving the service in 1993. *Weekly Mail,* 23 June 1995.

81. *New York Times,* 20 July 1991.

82. These and several other documents detailing the NP's support of Inkatha were leaked by Brian Morrow, a Durban security police officer. *Weekly Mail,* 19 July 1991; *Weekly Mail,* 23 December 1994.

83. Ibid.

84. Anthony Minnaar, "Hostels and Violent Conflict on the Reef," in *Communities in Isolation,* ed. Anthony Minnaar (Pretoria: Human Sciences Research Council, 1993), 15.

85. On Inkatha organizing in Soweto during the 1970s, see Philip Frankel, "The Politics of Poverty: Political Competition in Soweto," *Canadian Journal of African Studies* 14, no. 2 (1980). A 1985 MORI/Markinor (London) poll of Africans in the Durban metropolitan and Vaal Triangle areas found only six percent naming Buthelezi as South Africa's best leader or best future president, as compared to forty-nine percent naming Nelson Mandela. *Sunday Times,* 15 September 1985.

86. Reported by Inkatha defector Mbongeni Khumalo. *Weekly Mail,* 23 December 1992.

87. The training of Inkatha members was confirmed by Springbok Patrols' managing director Abraham Baartmann. *Weekly Mail,* 10 May 1991. Alexandra residents reported that the Inkatha members based in the hostels were unfamiliar with the township, suggesting that they had been brought in from elsewhere. *Weekly Mail,* 3 April 1992.

88. As many as five thousand men were reported to have been trained at the Mlaba facility. *Weekly Mail,* 15 April 1994.

89. Eugene de Kock, the commander of such a police unit, testified in 1996 to supplying Inkatha with a consignment of arms including 700 antitank mines, 1288 hand grenades, 182 rocket grenades, 308 mortars, 1428 rifle grenades, and 510kg of explosives. *Business Day,* 8 October 1996.

90. *Weekly Mail,* 15 April 1994.

Chapter 4

1. Lloyd A. Fallers, *Bantu Bureaucracy* (Chicago: University of Chicago Press, 1965); A. K. H. Weinrich, *Chiefs and Councils in Rhodesia* (London: Heinemann, 1971); J. F. Holleman, *Chief, Council, and Commissioner* (London: Oxford University Press, 1969).

2. Fallers, *Bantu Bureaucracy,* 239.

3. David Apter, *The Gold Coast in Transition* (Princeton: Princeton University Press, 1955), 365.

4. Mare and Hamilton, *An Appetite for Power,* 84.

5. Ibid.

6. Schlemmer, "The Stirring Giant," 115–16.

7. Mzala, *Gatsha Buthelezi,* 130.

8. Ibid.

9. Quoted in Mare and Hamilton, *An Appetite for Power,* 89.

10. Ben Temkin, *Gatsha Buthelezi: Zulu Statesman* (Cape Town: Purnell & Sons, 1976), 404. Mzala maintains, however, that no known Zulu tradition obliges kings to

appoint specified persons as advisors or prime ministers, and that although kings did select chief advisors, the position was not hereditary. Mzala, *Gatsha Buthelezi*, 105.

11. *Sunday Times*, 25 September 1994.

12. Butler et al., *The Black Homelands of South Africa*, 57; Mzala, *Gatsha Buthelezi*, 89–90.

13. See chapter 3.

14. KwaZulu Executive Council, "Role of the Zulu King," in *African Perspectives on South Africa*, ed. Hendrik van der Merwe, Nancy Charton, D. A. Kotze, and Ake Magnusson (Cape Town: David Philip, 1978), 470.

15. *Sunday Times*, 25 September 1994.

16. Loraine Gordon, *Survey of Race Relations in South Africa, 1979* (Johannesburg: South African Institute of Race Relations, 1980), 323; *Sunday Times*, 25 September 1994.

17. A memorandum distributed to teachers and principles in KwaZulu schools in 1978 stated: "The syllabus is based on the aims and objectives of the National Cultural Liberation Movement as found in the Constitution. . . . In drawing up this syllabus the committee was influenced by . . . the need to develop in our youth the whole person within the ambit of the Inkatha constitution . . . [and] that many adults seem to hold divergent views and beliefs about Inkatha . . . . These are passed on to the young and cloud the youths' minds. It is thus hoped that this syllabus together with its guide will clear many doubts and thus create unified ideas to match with the goals of Inkatha." Quoted in Praisley Mdluli [Blade Nzimande], "Ubuntu-Botho: Inkatha's Peoples' Education," *Transformation* 5 (1987), 65.

18. Ibid., 66.

19. *Rand Daily Mail*, 27 August 1976; *Rand Daily Mail*, 28 August 1976.

20. Gerhart, *Black Power in South Africa*, 258, 261.

21. Ibid., 269.

22. Inkatha, "Transcript, Meeting Between Chief Gatsha Buthelezi, President of Inkatha, and Mr. J. T. Kruger, Minister of Justice, Police and Prisons, at Union Buildings—Pretoria," 19 September 1977, document in the author's collection.

23. For example, in 1983 Buthelezi characterized popular resistance to the incorporation of Lamontville township into KwaZulu as an ethnic plot, stating, "We are sick and tired of people of Xhosa extraction here in our midst. . . . Lawyers, men of the cloth and people who penetrated our own organization, of Xhosa extraction, cannot be allowed the freedom in our midst to wreak havoc among our people and our youth." Mzala, *Gatsha Buthelezi*, 120.

24. *Ubuntu-Botho: Good Citizenship*, quoted in Mdluli, "Ubuntu-Botho," 69.

25. Ibid., 70.

26. Ibid.

27. Oscar Dhlomo, "Inkatha and the ANC," *Leadership SA* 3, no. 1 (1984), 47.

28. Mare and Hamilton, *An Appetite for Power*, 140–41.

29. Inkatha, *Letters from Black South Africans to the President of Inkatha*, undated document in the author's collection, 1–2.

30. Roger J. Southall, "Consociationalism in South Africa: the Buthelezi Commission and Beyond," *Journal of Modern African Studies* 21, no. 1 (1983), 84–85.

31. Daryl Glaser, "Behind the Indaba," *Transformation* 2 (1986), 5.

32. Ibid.; Southall, "Consociationalism in South Africa," 85.

33. Southall, "Consociationalism in South Africa," 85–86.

34. See Arendt Lijphart, *Democracy in Plural Societies* (New Haven: Yale University Press, 1977).

35. Buthelezi Commission, *The Requirements for Stability and Development in KwaZulu and Natal,* vol. 1 (Durban: H & H Publications, 1982), 12; Ibid., vol. 2, 106–16.

36. The ANC was formally invited to participate in the Indaba, but given its status as a banned organization, the invitation could hardly be taken seriously.

37. Peter Mansfield, "Checks and Balances," *Indaba* (1987), 37–38.

38. Karin Roberts and Graham Howe, *New Frontiers: The KwaZulu/Natal Debates* (Durban: University of Natal, 1987), 24.

39. Reproduced in Thomas Karis and Gwendolen Carter, *From Protest to Challenge,* vol. 1 (Stanford: Hoover Institution Press, 1972), 80–81.

40. Nelson Mandela, "Verwoerd's Tribalism," in *The Struggle is My Life* (New York: Pathfinder, 1990), 81.

41. Mbeki, *The Peasants' Revolt,* 47.

42. Thomas Karis and Gail Gerhart, *From Protest to Challenge,* vol. 5 (Bloomington: Indiana University Press, 1997), 32–33.

43. Ibid., 406–11.

44. "Further, as a weapon, the Bantustan scheme is intended to encourage and resuscitate the whole concept of tribalism, to keep it alive, firstly in South Africa and, later, in Africa itself. It is not inconceivable that Kenya, for instance, or even Zambia, and others will be receiving a long succession of groups who are Xhosas, Vendas, Tongas, various other names—calling themselves nations, where once before they were regarded as part of one nation. White South Africa is looking ahead. It is not happy with the unity of the African states under one leadership and the elimination of the tribal concept, which is colonialist in its origin. You don't hear of tribes in Europe, but we hear of tribes in Africa. It is a basis for division, and South Africa is forging this weapon." ANC, *Forward to Freedom,* 1975, African National Congress Library, Shell House, Johannesburg, South Africa.

45. "The Bantustan Fraud," *Sechaba,* 5 May 1969, reproduced in Aquino de Braganca and Immanuel Wallerstein, *The African Liberation Reader,* vol. 3, *The Strategy of Liberation* (London: Zed Press 1982), 10.

46. Mare and Hamilton, *An Appetite for Power,* 145.

47. Oliver R. Tambo, "Political Report of the National Executive Committee," speech delivered to the ANC National Consultative Conference, June 1985, quoted in Mzala, *Gatsha Buthelezi,* 127.

48. Rob Davies, Dan O'Meara, and Sipho Dlamini, *The Struggle For South Africa,* vol. 2 (London: Zed Books, 1985), 393.

49. ANC, "Report, Main Decisions and Recommendations of the Second National Consultative Conference, Lusaka, Zambia," 16–23 June 1985, African National Congress Library, Shell House, Johannesburg, South Africa.

50. See *New Nation,* 19 August 1987.

51. R. S. Ndou, interview by author, Johannesburg, South Africa, 7 December 1995.

52. Ibid.

53. Colleen McCaul, *Satellite in Revolt* (Johannesburg: South African Institute of Race Relations, 1987), 6.

54. R. S. Ndou, interview by author; *Weekly Mail,* 25 September 1987.

55. *Weekly Mail,* 25 September 1987.

56. ANC, "Joint Communiqué of a Meeting Between the ANC and COSATU," 19 August 1989, African National Congress Library, Shell House, Johannesburg, South Africa.

57. *Weekly Mail,* 7 October 1988. Notably, Inkatha's response to the ANC's constitutional guidelines (written by Secretary-General Oscar Dhlomo and published in the same issue of the *Weekly Mail*) made no mention of the proposed transformation of the institution of chieftaincy. Ibid.

58. ANC, *Ready to Govern: Policy Guidelines for a Democratic South Africa,* May 1992, sec. 3, African National Congress Library, Shell House, Johannesburg, South Africa.

59. Allen Isaacman and Barbara Isaacman, *Mozambique: From Colonialism to Revolution* (Boulder: Westview Press, 1983), 29.

60. Alex Vines, *RENAMO: Terrorism in Mozambique* (Bloomington: Indiana University Press, 1991), 5.

61. Quoted in William Finnegan, *A Complicated War* (Berkeley: University of California Press, 1992), 293.

62. Vines, *RENAMO,* 15, 18–19.

63. Finnegan, *A Complicated War,* 63; Vines, *RENAMO,* 92.

64. See Christian Geffray, *La Cause des Armes: Anthropologie de la Guerre Contemporaine au Mozambique* (Paris: Editions Karthala, 1990).

65. William Minter, *Apartheid's Contras* (Johannesburg: Witwatersrand University Press, 1994); Otto Roesch, "RENAMO and the Peasantry in Southern Mozambique," *Canadian Journal of African Studies* 26, no. 3 (1992).

66. Jeremy Cronin, interview by author, Johannesburg, South Africa, 30 October 1995.

67. Republic of South Africa, *House of Assembly Debates,* 6 May 1993, col. 7256.

68. *Sunday Times,* 31 October 1993.

Chapter 5

1. Arguments against the inclusion of separate IFP and KwaZulu delegations pointed out, however, that each Bantustan state was represented by either a ruling party or a government. Allowing the IFP to be seated as both a national political party and a Bantustan ruling party would have amounted to double representation.

2. *Weekly Mail,* 28 February 1992.

3. One such submission arrived from a man calling himself "His Majesty Maxhobayakhawuleza, Bangilizwe Sandile, King of the Ciskei Xhosa-speaking people." S. M. Burns-Ncamashe, "Memorandum to Rev. J. J. Mohapi, chairperson of the subcommittee on the King of the Zulus and other traditional leaders," 18 March 1992, African National Congress Library, Shell House, Johannesburg, South Africa. The claim to such a position is particularly interesting in light of Jeff Peires's well-evidenced argument that there exists no historical basis for a Ciskei Xhosa culture, as distinct from that of other Xhosa speakers. See [Jeff Peires], "Ethnicity and Pseudo-Ethnicity in the Ciskei."

4. *Weekly Mail,* 30 April 1992.

5. CODESA Working Group 2 Steering Committee, "General Constitutional Principles, Areas of Commonality," 12 May 1992, African National Congress Library, Shell House, Johannesburg, South Africa.

6. Republic of South Africa, Act 200 of 1993, sec. 181–83.

7. Charmaine French, "Functions and Powers of Traditional Leaders," *Konrad Adenauer Stiftung Occasional Papers*, September 1994, 21.

8. In exact correspondence with the shifting ideological strategies of indirect rule, what was originally known as the Native Affairs Department became the Department of Bantu Administration and Development (1959), the Department of Co-operation and Development (1979), and the Department of Development Aid (1985).

9. Department of Constitutional Development, *Traditional Leaders* (Pretoria: Republic of South Africa Government Printing Office, 1994). A larger number of sub-chiefs, classified as headmen in the Eastern Cape and as *izinduna* in KwaZulu-Natal, also held positions in the system, however, their numbers (probably between fifteen hundred and two thousand) remained in dispute.

10. N. Bromberger, "Some Socio-Economic Aspects of Vulindlela," in *Rural Studies in KwaZulu*, ed. N. Bromberger and J. D. Lea (Pietermaritzburg: University of Natal, 1982), 28.

11. Department of Constitutional Development, *Traditional Leaders*. At one meeting I was able to arrange with several chiefs from an area in Northern Natal, an elderly man arrived by public transportation wearing a threadbare coat, while another was chauffeured in his personal Mercedes-Benz, accompanied by armed bodyguards.

12. Inkatha Freedom Party, "Memorandum for Presentation to the President of South Africa, His Excellency Mr. Nelson Mandela," 22 December 1994, document in the author's collection, 6.

13. Nicholas Haysom, "Negotiating a Political Settlement in South Africa," in *South African Review 6*, ed. Glenn Moss and Ingrid Obery (Johannesburg: Ravan Press, 1992), 40.

14. Mangosuthu G. Buthelezi, *Fifth Session of the Fifth KwaZulu Legislative Assembly: Policy Speech by the Chief Minister of KwaZulu* (Ulundi: KwaZulu Legislative Assembly, 1993), 5.

15. Inkatha Freedom Party, "Memorandum for Presentation to the President of South Africa, His Excellency Mr. Nelson Mandela," 3.

16. Inkatha Freedom Party, "Memorandum for Presentation to the Minister of Provincial Affairs, Constitutional Development, and Local Government, the Hon. R. M. Meyer," 8 November 1994, document in the author's collection, 2. The obvious comparison is with the segregationist rhetoric of Heaton Nichols.

17. Inkatha Freedom Party, "Green Paper—Constitutional Principles," 3 October 1995, document in the author's collection, 33–34.

18. Ibid., 34.

19. *Human Rights Report* (Johannesburg: Human Rights Committee of South Africa, February 1996), 20.

20. *Business Day*, 13 May 1996.

21. Mhlabunzima Maphumulo, a Natal chief who had clashed with Buthelezi in the 1970s, was assassinated in 1991, two years after becoming president of CONTRALESA

and openly allying with the UDF. See Catharine Payze, "The Elimination of Political Opponents," in *Patterns of Violence*, ed. Anthony Minnaar (Pretoria: Human Sciences Research Council, 1992). Two other Natal chiefs, Elphas Molefe and Everson Xolo, were attacked and forced into hiding by IFP supporters after announcing their support for the ANC. *Africa Watch* 5, no. 12 (1993), 21; *Sunday Tribune*, April 28 1996.

22. KwaZulu-Natal Provincial Government, *Draft Constitution for the Province of KwaZulu-Natal*, 7 February 1996, document in the author's collection, 344. A quasi-historical argument was then devised to support this notion of a traditional constitutional monarch: "In the historical development of the Kingdom, the King of the Zulu Nation was transferred from an executive Monarch into a constitutional Monarch so that he could perform the function of unifying all the people of the Kingdom by symbolizing the historical aspirations of the Kingdom over and above any political division and present day politics." Inkatha Freedom Party, "Memorandum for Presentation to the President of South Africa, His Excellency Mr. Nelson Mandela," 2.

23. Chief Mhlabunzima Maphumulo, interview, *Sechaba* (May 1990), 8.

24. Patekile Holomisa, "Opening Address to the Customary Law Conference, Broederstroom, 16 July 1993," reproduced in *The Future of the Institution of Hereditary Rule and Customary Law in South Africa*, ed. R. S. Ndou and Essy M. Letsoalo (Johannesburg: CONTRALESA 1994), 6.

25. CONTRALESA, "Memorandum to CODESA Management Committee," 27 January 1991, African National Congress Library, Shell House, Johannesburg, South Africa, 5.

26. CONTRALESA, "Press Release," 18 March 1995, African National Congress Library, Shell House, Johannesburg, South Africa, 2.

27. Patekile Holomisa, "The Role of Traditional Leaders in Local Government," (speech delivered at the Konrad Adenauer Stiftung workshop on Traditional Leaders in Local Government, Durban, 27–28 October 1994), reproduced in *Seminar Report* (Johannesburg: Konrad Adenauer Stiftung 1994), 39.

28. CONTRALESA, "Press Release," 18 March 1995, 2.

29. R. S. Ndou, interview by author, Johannesburg, South Africa, 7 December 1995.

30. Ibid.

31. *Weekly Mail*, 24 November 1989. Rumors that unity talks were underway between CONTRALESA and the IFP were confirmed when Holomisa and Buthelezi appeared together at a demonstration in Pretoria on 28 October 1995.

32. *Weekly Mail*, 18 November 1994.

33. *Mercury*, 15 March 1996.

34. See, for example, Nelson Mandela's comments in Mamphela Ramphele, *A Life* (Johannesburg: Ravan Press, 1995), 203.

35. "Since authority always demands obedience, it is commonly mistaken for some form of power or violence. Yet authority precludes the use of external means of coercion; where force is used, authority itself has failed. Authority, on the other hand, is incompatible with persuasion, which presupposes equality and works through a process of argumentation. Where arguments are used authority is left in abeyance. . . . If authority is to be defined at all, then, it must be in contradistinction to both coercion by force and persuasion through arguments." Hannah Arendt, "What is Authority?" in *Between Past and Future* (New York: Penguin Books, 1977), 93.

36. Ibid., 91.

37. Inkatha Freedom Party, "Memorandum for Presentation to Pres. N. R. Mandela submitted by a Delegation of Traditional Leaders of South Africa," 28 October 1995, document in the author's collection, 1.

38. Arendt, "What is Authority?" 120.

39. Ibid., 124.

40. CONTRALESA, "Memorandum to CODESA Management Committee," 27 January 1991, 3.

41. IFP: "Memorandum for Presentation to the President of South Africa, His Excellency Mr. Nelson Mandela," 22 December 1994, 6.

42. Inkatha Freedom Party, "Meeting of the Amakhosi of the Kingdom of KwaZulu-Natal, Members of the Zulu Royal House, and Members of Iso Lesizwe," 28 July 1995, document in the author's collection, 1.

43. Ironically, the extreme distances from which people were bussed to attend the refounding meant that most of the crowd had left for home before the covenant was actually read. Events observed by the author, 20 August 1995.

44. Arendt, "What is Authority?" 122.

45. Hanna Pitkin, *The Concept of Representation* (Berkeley: University of California Press, 1967), 32.

46. In the middle 1980s, community-based activists interested in developing a system of direct democracy through township civic associations strongly criticized the standard liberal model of representative democracy. During the height of the anti-apartheid struggle, the civic associations were largely in control of several major urban townships. See Mzwanele Mayekiso, *Township Politics: Civic Struggles for a New South Africa* (New York: Monthly Review Press, 1996). Trade unions organized by COSATU also maintained highly participatory models of democracy in which representatives operated only under strict mandates defined by mass meetings of rank-and-file members.

47. CONTRALESA, "Constitution," 1991, African National Congress Library, Shell House, Johannesburg, South Africa.

48. IFP: "Memorandum for Presentation to Pres. N. R. Mandela submitted by a Delegation of Traditional Leaders of South Africa," 28 October 1995, 1.

49. Patekile Holomisa, "Opening Address to the Customary Law Conference," p. 9.

50. One study of a Transkei community during the late 1980s described the *pitso* as having become little more than a means of transmitting orders from the tribal authority and squelching dissent. People in the community were reported to have regarded the *pitso* as a "waste of time." Segar, *Fruits of Apartheid*, 31, 134. A study of chieftaincy in KwaZulu, also conducted during the late 1980s, reported that even in the community of a chief who appeared to value consensus, *izimbizo* were infrequent. Graham Inglis Callanan, "Portrait of a Zulu Chief" (BA Honours Thesis, University of Natal-Durban, 1986), 134. An earlier study of chieftaincy in KwaZulu was even more critical of the notion that the system operated by consensus. "The structure of the system, however, does not lend itself to consensus democracy. Legislation governing the functions of the chiefs does not require them to consult their people when taking important decisions—at best the chief is supposed to consult his councilors who are all his own appointees." Paul Daphne, "Tribal Authority

and Community Organization," University of Zululand Occasional Papers, no. 3 (1982), 7.

51. Pitkin, *The Concept of Representation*, 53.

52. Michael Sutcliffe, interview with author, Durban, South Africa, 27 October 1995.

53. Pitkin, *The Concept of Representation*, 103.

54. Joseph Masangu, interview with author, Durban, South Africa, 30 August 1995.

55. CONTRALESA, "Memorandum to CODESA Management Committee," 27 January 1991, 6; Herbert W. Vilikazi, "Thoughts on How to Build a Nation and a Lasting Constitution," Submission to CODESA Management Committee on the Zulu King, 12 March 1992, African National Congress Library, Shell House, Johannesburg, South Africa, 14–15.

56. Eric Hobsbawm, "Identity Politics and the Left," *New Left Review*, no. 217 (May/June 1996), 38–39.

57. Pitkin, *The Concept of Representation*, 60–63.

58. Robert Knox, *The Races of Men* (London: Henry Renshaw, 1850), 56.

59. Mario Oriano-Ambrosini, interview, *Rethinking Rights*, no. 1 (Summer 1993), 27.

60. *Weekly Mail*, 26 May 1995.

61. *Sunday Independent*, 5 May 1996.

62. CONTRALESA, "Press Release," 18 March 1995, 2.

63. Rudi Hillerman (member of the Durban Demarcation Board), interview with author, Durban, South Africa, 30 November 1995.

64. Ibid.; *Mercury*, 27 January 1995.

65. N. Bromberger, "Some Socio-Economic Aspects of Vulindlela," 39.

66. Ibid., 53.

67. Catherine Cross, "Informal Tenures Against the State: Landholding Systems in African Rural Areas," in *A Harvest of Discontent: The Land Question in South Africa*, ed. Michael de Klerk (Cape Town: IDASA, 1991), 74.

68. Callanan, "Portrait of a Zulu Chief," 106–7.

69. Buthelezi, "Policy Speech," 76.

70. Union of South Africa, Act 21 of 1923, sec. 27b.

71. KwaZulu, Act 16 of 1985, sec. 3, 14. Callanan's study reports a chief's prosecution of a man for illegally carrying a shield, spear, and sharpened stick. Callanan, "Portrait of a Zulu Chief," 136.

72. Republic of South Africa, Proclamation R164 of 1990.

73. Police officer Eugene de Kock testified in 1996 that he was instructed by his commander to file a false claim form for R20,000 so that the funds could be used to "manufacture assegais [spears] for the Zulus." *Mail & Guardian*, 20 September 1996.

74. Events of 4 May 1996, observed by the author.

75. Catherine Campbell, Gerhard Mare, and Cherryl Walker, "Evidence for an Ethnic Identity in the Life Histories of Zulu-Speaking Durban Township Residents," *Journal of Southern African Studies* 21, no. 2 (June 1995).

76. Ibid., 292.

77. NAD correspondence files, vol. 8993, 214/362, National Archives, Pretoria, South Africa.

78. See Eddy Maloka, "Traditional Leaders and the Current Transition," *The African Communist*, no. 141 (Second Quarter 1995). SANCO activists were frequently critical of traditional authority and called for the legitimacy of individual traditional leaders to be tested by referendum.

79. Peter Rutsch, "Traditional Trauma," *Indicator SA* 12, no. 2 (Autumn 1995), 35.

80. Zola S. T. Skweyiya, "Chieftaincy, the Ethnic Question and the Democratisation Process in South Africa," Community Law Centre, University of the Western Cape Occasional Papers (March 1993), 5.

81. J. C. Bekker, "Tribal Government at the Crossroads," *Africa Insight* 21, no. 2 (1991), 131.

82. Patekile Holomisa, "The Role of Traditional Leaders in Local Government," 37.

83. Alastair McIntosh, "Rethinking Chieftaincy and the Future of Rural Local Government," *Transformation* 13 (1990), 33. Works cited by McIntosh: D. L. Dlamini, "The Role of the Chief's Court in KwaZulu" (PhD Thesis, University of Zululand, 1987); M. Marais, *The Dynamics of Change at the Local Level* (Durban: Inkatha Institute, 1989).

84. Richard J. Haines and C. P. Tapscott, "The Silence of Poverty: Tribal Administration and Development in Rural Transkei," in *Towards Freehold: Options for Land & Development in South Africa's Black Rural Areas*, ed. Catherine Cross and Richard Haines (Cape Town: Juta & Company, 1988), 169.

85. Paulus M. Zulu, "An Identification of Base-Line Socio-Political Structures in Rural Areas, Their Operation and Potential Role in Community Development in KwaZulu," University of Zululand Occasional Paper (1984), 9.

86. Haines and Tapscott, "The Silence of Poverty," 170.

87. Paulus M. Zulu, "The Rural Crisis: Authority Structures and their Role in Development," in *Up Against the Fences: Poverty, Passes and Privilege in South Africa*, ed. Hermann Giliomee and Lawrence Schlemmer (Cape Town: David Philip, 1985), 244.

88. Zulu, "An Identification of Base-Line Socio-Political Structures," 12.

89. Ibid., 13.

90. Haines and Tapscott, "The Silence of Poverty," 170.

91. Tessa Marcus, Kathy Eales, and Adele Wildschut, *Down to Earth: Land Demand in the New South Africa* (Durban: Indicator Press, 1996), 87–88.

92. Zulu, "An Identification of Base-Line Socio-Political Structures," 22.

93. Ibid., 23.

94. The KwaZulu Legislative Assembly voted in 1976 to impose fines of up to R200 for the crime of insolence to a chief. Mare and Hamilton, *An Appetite for Power*, 89.

95. Callanan, "Portrait of a Zulu Chief," 122.

96. Karl Marx, *Capital*, vol. 1, trans. Ben Fowkes (New York: Vintage Books, 1977), 165.

97. Slavoj Zizek, *The Sublime Object of Ideology* (New York: Verso, 1989), 11.

98. Sigmund Freud, *The Interpretation of Dreams* (New York: Basic Books, 1955), 506–7.

99. Zizek, *The Sublime Object of Ideology*, 34.

100. Pitkin, *The Concept of Representation*, 236.

101. Marx, *Capital*, vol. 1, 149n22. Not all hereditary rulers fail to comprehend the relational aspect of their position. One South African chief expressed his opposition to a government program to improve low-income housing saying, "If the government builds people houses and the people have better houses than [the chiefs], they will begin to undermine us." *Weekly Mail*, 7 July 1995. Similar complaints were lodged by CONTRALESA against South Africa's 1993 interim constitution. The organization's leaders held that allocating the House of Traditional Leaders merely an advisory role would have the effect of undermining the legitimacy of chieftaincy. CONTRALESA: "Press Release," 18 March 1995, 3.

102. John Comaroff, "Rules and Roles: Political Processes in a Tswana Chiefdom," in *Working Papers in Southern African Studies*, ed. P. L. Bonner (Johannesburg: African Studies Institute, University of the Witwatersrand, 1979).

103. Consider, for example, the difficulties faced by those who attempt to counterfeit the active authorization of democratic elections. Even after stuffing ballot boxes or conspiring with election officials, the potential for doubt and disbelief on the part of citizens (who know that they have not voted for the winner of the contest) is enormous.

104. D. H. Reader, *Zulu Tribe in Transition* (Manchester: Manchester University Press, 1966), 253.

105. Republic of South Africa, *House of Assembly Debates*, 14 November 1994, col. 4237.

Epilogue

1. Republic of South Africa, *Constitution of the Republic of South Africa* (1996), chap. 12.

2. *Mail & Guardian*, 6 October 2000.

3. Department of Provincial and Local Government, *White Paper on Traditional Leadership and Governance*, Notice 2336 (Pretoria: Republic of South Africa Government Printing Office, 2003).

4. Republic of South Africa, Act 41 of 2003, sec. 28.

5. Ibid., sec. 11–12.

6. Ibid., sec. 19–20.

7. Ibid., sec. 3–4.

8. Lodge, *Black Politics in South Africa Since 1945*, 71.

9. Gerhart, *Black Power in South Africa*, 146.

10. ANC, *Forward to Freedom*, 1975, African National Congress Library, Shell House, Johannesburg, South Africa, 1.

11. Stephen Ellis and Tsepo Sechaba, *Comrades Against Apartheid* (Bloomington: Indiana University Press, 1992), 122.

12. Department of Provincial and Local Government, *White Paper on Traditional Leadership and Governance*, 20–22.

13. Ibid., 31–32, 47, 52.

14. Republic of South Africa, *Land Restitution in South Africa: Our Achievements and Challenges* (Pretoria: Republic of South Africa Government Printing Office, 2003).

15. Alastair McIntosh, Sipho Sibanda, Anne Vaughan, and Thokozani Xaba, *Traditional Authorities and Land: The Position in KwaZulu Natal* (Pietermaritzburg: Association for Rural Advancement, 1995), 9.

16. Tom Nevin, "Land: A Tale of Two Countries," *African Business* (April 2004), 28.

17. *Mail & Guardian*, 24 July 2003.

18. *Mail & Guardian*, 23 November 2001; Nevin, "Land," 29.

19. Republic of South Africa, Act 11 of 2004, sec. 2, 5–6.

20. Ibid., sec. 21.

21. Ibid., sec. 26.

22. *Mercury*, 22 July 2004; *Sunday Independent*, 23 April 2006.

23. *Mail & Guardian*, 29 January 2003.

24. *Mercury*, 23 May 2005.

25. *Mercury*, 25 May 2005.

26. Jacob Zuma, "Address By Deputy President Jacob Zuma at the Official Handover of the Community Based Public Works Programme Projects by the Nkangala District Municipality Klipfontein, Mpumalanga, 18 December 2004," African National Congress, http://www.anc.org.za/ancdocs/history/zuma/2004/jz1218.html.

27. *Daily Dispatch*, 11 April 2006.

28. *Mercury*, 7 July 2006.

29. National House of Traditional Leaders, "Statement on the Resolutions of the National Annual Conference of Traditional Leaders," Republic of South Africa, 9 December 2005, http://www.info.gov.za/speeches/2005/05120914151004.htm.

Selected Bibliography

This bibliography includes all secondary sources referred to in the text, as well as a list of newspapers and periodicals from which articles have been cited. Full citations for primary source material are provided in the notes.

Newspapers and Periodicals

Business Day, Johannesburg
Cape Times, Cape Town
Daily Dispatch, East London
Daily News, Durban
Mercury, Durban
Natal Witness, Pietermaritzburg
New Nation, Johannesburg
New York Times, New York
Rand Daily Mail, Johannesburg
Saturday Paper, Durban
Sowetan, Johannesburg
Star, Johannesburg
Sunday Independent, Johannesburg
Sunday Times, Johannesburg
Sunday Tribune, Durban
Weekly Mail/Mail & Guardian, Johannesburg

Secondary Sources

Aitchison, John. "The Civil War in Natal." In *South African Review* 5, edited by G. Moss and I. Obery. Johannesburg: Ravan Press, 1989.
———. *The Seven Days War: 25–31 March, 1990*. Pietermaritzburg: University of Natal Centre for Adult Education, 1990.
Alcock, Creina. "Impi." *Leadership South Africa* 7, no. 1 (1988).
Althusser, Louis. *Lenin and Philosophy*. New York: Monthly Review Press, 1971.
Apter, David. *The Gold Coast in Transition*. Princeton: Princeton University Press, 1955.

Arendt, Hannah. *Between Past and Future.* New York: Penguin Books, 1977.

Ashforth, Adam. *The Politics of Official Discourse.* Oxford: Oxford University Press, 1990.

Baskin, Jeremy. *Striking Back: A History of COSATU.* London: Verso, 1991.

Beinart, William. *The Political Economy of Pondoland, 1860 to 1930.* Johannesburg: Ravan Press, 1982.

———. "Chieftaincy and the Concept of Articulation." In *Segregation and Apartheid in Twentieth-Century South Africa,* edited by William Beinart and Saul Dubow. London: Routledge, 1995.

Bekker, J. C. "Tribal Government at the Crossroads." *Africa Insight* 21, no. 2 (1991).

Bennett, T. W. *A Sourcebook of African Customary Law for Southern Africa.* Cape Town: Juta & Company, 1991.

Boahen, A. Adu. *Africa Under Colonial Domination, 1880–1935.* Paris: UNESCO, 1990.

Bonner, Philip. "The Transvaal Native Congress 1917–20." In *Industrialization and Social Change in South Africa,* edited by Shula Marks and Richard Rathbone. New York: Longman, 1982.

Brewer, John D. "The Membership of Inkatha in Kwamashu." *African Affairs* 84, no. 334 (1985).

Bromberger, N. "Some Socio-Economic Aspects of Vulindlela." In *Rural Studies in KwaZulu,* edited by N. Bromberger and J. D. Lea. Pietermaritzburg: University of Natal, 1982.

Brookes, Edgar. *The History of Native Policy in South Africa.* Pretoria: J. L. Van Schaik, 1927.

Brooks, Alan, and Jeremy Brickhill. *Whirlwind Before the Storm.* London: International Defence and Aid Fund for Southern Africa, 1980.

Bundy, Colin. "Land and Liberation." In *The Politics of Race, Class and Nationalism in 20th Century South Africa,* edited by Shula Marks and Stanley Trapido. London: Longman, 1987.

———. *The Rise & Fall of the South African Peasantry.* Cape Town: David Philip, 1988.

Buthelezi Commission. *The Requirements for Stability and Development in KwaZulu and Natal.* 2 vols. Durban: H & H Publications, 1982.

Butler, Jeffrey, Robert I. Rotberg, and John Adams. *The Black Homelands of South Africa.* Berkeley: University of California Press, 1977.

Callanan, Graham Inglis. "Portrait of a Zulu Chief." BA Honours Thesis, University of Natal-Durban, 1986.

Campbell, Catherine, Gerhard Mare, and Cherryl Walker. "Evidence for an Ethnic Identity in the Life Histories of Zulu-Speaking Durban Township Residents." *Journal of Southern African Studies* 21, no. 2 (1995).

Carter, Gwendolen M., Thomas Karis, and Newell M. Stultz. *South Africa's Transkei.* Evanston: Northwestern University Press, 1967.

Catholic Institute for International Relations. *Now Everyone is Afraid.* London: CIRR, 1988.

Cell, John. *The Highest Stage of White Supremacy.* Cambridge: Cambridge University Press, 1982.

Cohen, G. A. *Karl Marx's Theory of History: A Defence.* Princeton: Princeton University Press, 1978.

Comaroff, John L. "Chiefship in a South African Homeland." *Journal of Southern African Studies* 1, no. 1 (1974).

———. "Rules and Roles: Political Processes in a Tswana Chiefdom." In *Working Papers in Southern African Studies*, edited by P. L. Bonner. Johannesburg: African Studies Institute, University of the Witwatersrand, 1979.

Comninel, George C. *Rethinking the French Revolution*. New York: Verso, 1987.

Cope, Nicholas. *To Bind the Nation*. Pietermaritzburg: University of Natal Press, 1993.

Coplan, David. "The Emergence of an African Working-Class Culture." In *Industrialization and Social Change in South Africa*, edited by Shula Marks and Richard Rathbone. New York: Longman, 1982.

Cross, Catherine. "Informal Tenures Against the State: Landholding Systems in African Rural Areas." In *A Harvest of Discontent: The Land Question in South Africa*, edited by Michael de Klerk. Cape Town: IDASA, 1991.

Cross, Catherine, and Richard Haines, eds. *Towards Freehold: Options for Land & Development in South Africa's Black Rural Areas*. Cape Town: Juta & Company, 1988.

Daphne, Paul. "Tribal Authority and Community Organization." University of Zululand Occasional Papers, no. 3 (1982).

Davies, Rob, Dan O' Meara, and Sipho Dlamini. *The Struggle For South Africa*. 2 vols. London: Zed Books, 1985.

De Braganca, Aquino, and Immanuel Wallerstein, eds. *The African Liberation Reader*. Vol. 3, *The Strategy of Liberation*. London: Zed Press, 1982.

Dhlomo, Oscar. "Inkatha and the ANC." *Leadership SA* 3, no. 1 (1984).

Dubow, Saul. *Racial Segregation and the Origins of Apartheid*. London: Macmillan Press, 1989.

Du Plessis, Lourens. "Covert Operations: Front Companies." In *The Hidden Hand: Covert Operations in South Africa*, edited by Anthony Minnaar, Ian Liebenberg, and Charl Schutte. Pretoria: Human Sciences Research Council, 1994.

Eagleton, Terry. *Ideology*. New York: Verso, 1991.

Ellis, Stephen, and Tsepo Sechaba. *Comrades Against Apartheid*. Bloomington: Indiana University Press, 1992.

Engels, Frederick. *The Origin of the Family, Private Property, and the State*. New York: International Publishers, 1968.

Etherington, Norman. "The 'Shepstone System' in the Colony of Natal and Beyond the Borders." In *Natal and Zululand from Earliest Times to 1910*, edited by Andrew Duminy and Bill Guest. Pietermaritzburg: University of Natal Press, 1989.

Fallers, Lloyd A. *Bantu Bureaucracy*. Chicago: University of Chicago Press, 1965.

Finnegan, William. *A Complicated War*. Berkeley: University of California Press, 1992.

Frankel, Philip. "The Politics of Poverty: Political Competition in Soweto." *Canadian Journal of African Studies* 14, no. 2 (1980).

French, Charmaine. "Functions and Powers of Traditional Leaders." Konrad Adenauer Stiftung Occasional Papers (September 1994).

Freud, Sigmund. *The Interpretation of Dreams*. New York: Basic Books, 1955.

Geffray, Christian. *La Cause des Armes: Anthropologie de la Guerre Contemporaine au Mozambique*. Paris: Editions Karthala, 1990.

Gerhart, Gail M. *Black Power in South Africa: The Evolution of an Ideology*. Berkeley: University of California Press, 1978.

Girvin, S. D. "Race and Race Classification." In *Race and the Law in South Africa*, edited by A. Rycroft. Cape Town: Juta & Company, 1987.

Glaser, Daryl. "Behind the Indaba." *Transformation* 2 (1986).

Gordon, Loraine. *Survey of Race Relations in South Africa, 1979.* Johannesburg: South African Institute of Race Relations, 1980.

Gramsci, Antonio. *Selections from the Prison Notebooks.* Translated and edited by Quentin Hoare and Geoffrey Nowell Smith. New York: International Publishers, 1971.

Guy, Jeff. "The Destruction and Reconstruction of Zulu Society." In *Industrialization and Social Change in South Africa*, edited by Shula Marks and Richard Rathbone. New York: Longman, 1982.

———. *The Destruction of the Zulu Kingdom.* Pietermaritzburg: University of Natal Press, 1994.

Haines, Richard J., and C. P. Tapscott. "The Silence of Poverty: Tribal Administration and Development in Rural Transkei." In *Towards Freehold: Options for Land & Development in South Africa's Black Rural Areas*, edited by Catherine Cross and Richard Haines. Cape Town: Juta & Company, 1988.

Hammond-Tooke, David. *Command or Consensus.* Cape Town: David Philip, 1975.

Haysom, Nicholas. *Mabangalala.* Johannesburg: University of the Witwatersrand Centre for Applied Legal Studies, Occasional Paper 10 (1986).

———. "Negotiating a Political Settlement in South Africa." In *South African Review 6*, edited by Glenn Moss and Ingrid Obery. Johannesburg: Ravan Press, 1992.

Hobsbawm, Eric. "Identity Politics and the Left." *New Left Review*, n. 217 (May/June 1996).

Holleman, J. F. *Chief, Council, and Commissioner.* London: Oxford University Press, 1969.

Horowitz, Donald L. "The Beginning of the End." *New Republic* 26 (November 1990).

———. *A Democratic South Africa?* Berkeley: University of California Press, 1991.

Horrell, Muriel. *Legislation and Race Relations.* Johannesburg: South African Institute of Race Relations, 1971.

Isaacman, Allen, and Barbara Isaacman. *Mozambique: From Colonialism to Revolution.* Boulder: Westview Press, 1983.

Kane-Berman, John. "Inkatha: The Paradox of South African Politics." *Optima* 30 (1982).

Karis, Thomas G., and Gwendolen Carter. *From Protest to Challenge.* Vol. 1. Stanford: Hoover Institution Press, 1972.

Karis, Thomas G., and Gail M. Gerhart. *From Protest to Challenge.* Vol. 5. Bloomington: Indiana University Press, 1997.

Knox, Robert. *The Races of Men.* London: Henry Renshaw, 1850.

Lacey, Marian. *Working for Boroko.* Johannesburg: Ravan Press, 1981.

Lambert, John. "Chiefship in Early Colonial Natal." *Journal of Southern African Studies* 21, no. 2 (1995).

Lapping, Brian. *Apartheid—A History.* New York: George Braziller, 1987.

Legassick, Martin. "Legislation, Ideology, and Economy in Post–1948 South Africa." *Journal of Southern African Studies* 1, no. 1 (1974).

Lijphart, Arendt. *Democracy in Plural Societies.* New Haven: Yale University Press, 1977.

Lodge, Tom. *Black Politics in South Africa Since 1945.* Johannesburg: Ravan Press, 1983.

Machiavelli, Niccolo. *The Prince.* Translated by George Bull. London: Penguin Books, 1999.

Mafeje, Archie. "An African Chief Visits Town." *Journal of Local Administration Overseas* 2, no. 2 (1963).

Maloka, Eddy. "Traditional Leaders and the Current Transition." *The African Communist*, no. 141 (1995).

Mamdani, Mahmood. *Citizen and Subject*. Princeton: Princeton University Press, 1996.

Mandela, Nelson. *The Struggle is My Life*. New York: Pathfinder, 1990.

Mansfield, Peter. "Checks and Balances." *Indaba* (1987).

Maphumulo, Mhlabunzima. "Interview." *Sechaba* (May 1990).

Marcus, Tessa, Kathy Eales, and Adele Wildschut. *Down to Earth: Land Demand in the New South Africa*. Durban: Indicator Press, 1996.

Mare, Gerhard. *African Population Relocation in South Africa*. Johannesburg: South African Institute of Race Relations, 1980.

Mare, Gerhard, and Georgina Hamilton. *An Appetite for Power: Buthelezi's Inkatha and the Politics of Loyal Resistance*. Johannesburg: Ravan Press, 1987.

Marks, Shula. *The Ambiguities of Dependence in South Africa*. Johannesburg: Ravan Press, 1986.

Marx, Karl. *Capital*. Vol. 1. Translated by Ben Fowkes. New York: Vintage Books, 1977.

———. "Preface to *A Contribution to the Critique of Political Economy*." In *The Marx-Engels Reader*. Edited by Robert C. Tucker. New York: Norton, 1978.

———. *Later Political Writings*. Translated and edited by Terrell Carver. Cambridge: Cambridge University Press, 1996.

Mayekiso, Mzwanele. *Township Politics: Civic Struggles for a New South Africa*. New York: Monthly Review Press, 1996.

Mbeki, Govan. *The Peasants' Revolt*. London: International Defence and Aid Fund for Southern Africa, 1984.

McCaul, Colleen. *Satellite in Revolt*. Johannesburg: South African Institute of Race Relations, 1987.

McCoy, James W. *Secrets of the Viet Cong*. New York: Hippocrene Books, 1992.

McCuen, John J. *The Art of Counter-Revolutionary War*. Harrisburg: Stackpole Books, 1966.

McIntosh, Alastair. "Rethinking Chieftaincy and the Future of Rural Local Government." *Transformation* 13 (1990).

McIntosh, Alastair, Sipho Sibanda, Anne Vaughan, and Thokozani Xaba. *Traditional Authorities and Land: The Position in KwaZulu Natal*. Pietermaritzburg: Association for Rural Advancement, 1995.

Mdluli, Praisley [Blade Nzimande]. "Ubuntu-Botho: Inkatha's Peoples' Education." *Transformation* 5 (1987).

Miles, Robert. *Racism After "Race Relations."* New York: Routledge, 1993.

Minnaar, Anthony. *Conflict and Violence in Natal/Kwazulu*. Pretoria: Human Sciences Research Council, 1991.

———. "Undisputed Kings: Warlordism in Natal." In *Patterns of Violence*, edited by Anthony Minnaar. Pretoria: Human Sciences Research Council, 1992.

———. "Hostels and Violent Conflict on the Reef." In *Communities in Isolation: Perspectives on Hostels in South Africa*, edited by Anthony Minnaar. Pretoria: Human Sciences Research Council, 1993.

Minter, William. *Apartheid's Contras*. Johannesburg: Witwatersrand University Press, 1994.

Mkhondo, Rich. *Reporting South Africa.* London: James Currey, 1993.

Mohapeloa, J. M. *Africans and Their Chiefs.* Cape Town: African Bookman, 1945.

Montsitsi, Sechaba, and 'Prof' Morobe. "Interview." *SASRU Focus* 2, no. 2 (June 1983).

Mufson, Steven. *Fighting Years: Black Resistance and the Struggle for a New South Africa.* Boston: Beacon Press, 1990.

Mzala. *Gatsha Buthelezi: Chief with a Double Agenda.* London: Zed Books, 1988.

Ndou, R. S., and Essy M. Letsoalo, eds. *The Future of the Institution of Hereditary Rule and Customary Law in South Africa.* Johannesburg: CONTRALESA, 1994.

Nevin, Tom. "Land: A Tale of Two Countries." *African Business* (April 2004).

Norval, Aletta J. *Deconstructing Apartheid Discourse.* New York: Verso, 1996.

Olivier, Johan L. "Political Conflict in South Africa: A Resource Mobilization Approach." In *Capturing the Event: Conflict Trends in the Natal Region 1986–1992,* edited by Simon Bekker. Durban: Centre for Social and Development Studies, University of Natal, 1992.

Oriano-Ambrosini, Mario. "Interview." *Rethinking Rights,* no. 1 (Summer 1993).

Pakenham, Thomas. *The Scramble for Africa.* New York: Random House, 1991.

Payze, Catharine. "The Elimination of Political Opponents." In *Patterns of Violence,* edited by Anthony Minnaar. Pretoria: Human Sciences Research Council, 1992.

[Peires, J. B.] "Ethnicity and Pseudo-Ethnicity in the Ciskei." In *The Creation of Tribalism in Southern Africa,* edited by Leroy Vail. Berkeley: University of California Press, 1989.

Peires, J. B. "The Implosion of Transkei and Ciskei." *African Affairs* 91 (1992).

Pitkin, Hanna. *The Concept of Representation.* Berkeley: University of California Press, 1967.

Posel, Deborah. "The Meaning of Apartheid before 1948." *Journal of Southern African Studies* 14 (1987).

Poulantzas, Nicos. *Political Power & Social Classes.* London: Verso, 1978.

Powell, Ivor. "Aspects of Propaganda Operations." In *The Hidden Hand: Covert Operations in South Africa,* edited by Anthony Minnaar, Ian Liebenberg, and Charl Schutte. Pretoria: Human Sciences Research Council, 1994.

Price, Robert M. *The Apartheid State in Crisis.* New York: Oxford University Press, 1991.

Radcliffe-Brown, A. R. "Some Problems of Bantu Sociology." *Bantu Studies* 1 (1921–22).

Ramphele, Mamphela. *A Life.* Johannesburg: Ravan Press, 1995.

Reader, D. H. *Zulu Tribe in Transition.* Manchester: Manchester University Press, 1966.

Ritchken, Edwin. "The KwaNdebele Struggle Against Independence." In *South African Review* 5, edited by Glenn Moss and Ingrid Obery. Johannesburg: Ravan Press, 1989.

Roberts, Karin, and Graham Howe. *New Frontiers: The KwaZulu/Natal Debates.* Durban: University of Natal, 1987.

Roesch, Otto. "RENAMO and the Peasantry in Southern Mozambique." *Canadian Journal of African Studies* 26, no. 3 (1992).

Rogers, Howard. *Native Administration in the Union of South Africa.* Johannesburg: University of the Witwatersrand Press, 1933.

Roth, Mirjana. "Elections under the Representation of Natives Act." In *Resistance and Ideology in Settler Societies,* edited by Tom Lodge. Johannesburg: Ravan Press, 1986.

Rousseau, Jean-Jacques. *The Basic Political Writings.* Translated and edited by Donald A. Cress. Indianapolis: Hackett, 1987.

Rutsch, Peter. "Traditional Trauma." *Indicator SA* 12, no. 2 (Autumn 1995).

Schapera, Isaac, ed. *The Bantu-Speaking Tribes of South Africa,* London: Routledge, 1937.

———. *Government and Politics in Tribal Societies.* London: Watts & Company, 1956.

Schlemmer, Lawrence. "The Stirring Giant: Observations on the Inkatha and Other Black Political Movements in South Africa." In *The Apartheid Regime: Political Power and Racial Domination,* edited by Robert M. Price and Carl G. Rosberg. Berkeley: Institute of International Studies, 1980.

Segar, Julia. *Fruits of Apartheid.* Bellville: Anthropos Publishers, 1989.

Skweyiya, Zola S. T. "Chieftaincy, the Ethnic Question and the Democratisation Process in South Africa." Community Law Centre, University of the Western Cape Occasional Papers (March 1993).

Southall, Roger. "Buthelezi, Inkatha and the Politics of Compromise." *African Affairs* 80, no. 321 (1981).

———. "Consociationalism in South Africa: The Buthelezi Commission and Beyond." *Journal of Modern African Studies* 21, no. 1 (1983).

———. *South Africa's Transkei.* New York: Monthly Review Press, 1983.

Stockwell, John. In *Search of Enemies.* New York: W. W. Norton & Company, 1978.

Stultz, Newell M. "Some Implications of African 'Homelands' in South Africa." In *The Apartheid Regime,* edited by Robert M. Price and Carl G. Rosberg. Berkeley: Institute of International Studies, 1980.

Sutcliffe, Michael, and Paul Wellings. "Inkatha Versus the Rest." *African Affairs* 87, no. 348 (1988).

Suzman, Arthur. "Race Classification and Definition in the Legislation of the Union of South Africa, 1910–1960." *Acta Juridica* 342 (1960).

Tabata, I. B. *The All African Convention: The Awakening of a People.* Johannesburg: People's Press, 1950.

Taylor, Rupert. "The Myth of Ethnic Division: Township Conflict on the Reef." *Race and Class* 33, no. 2 (1991).

Temkin, Ben. *Gatsha Buthelezi: Zulu Statesman.* Cape Town: Purnell & Sons, 1976.

Thompson, Edward P. "Eighteenth-Century English Society: Class Struggle without Class?" *Social History* 3, no. 2 (1978).

Tignor, Robert. "Colonial Chiefs in Chiefless Societies." *Journal of Modern African Studies* 9, no. 3 (1971).

Van der Merwe, Hendrik, Nancy Charton, D. A. Kotze, and Ake Magnusson, eds. *African Perspectives on South Africa.* Cape Town: David Philip, 1978.

Van Warmelo, N. J. *A Preliminary Survey of the Bantu Tribes of South Africa.* Pretoria: Department of Native Affairs, 1935.

Vines, Alex. *RENAMO: Terrorism in Mozambique.* Bloomington: Indiana University Press, 1991.

Webb, C. de B., and J. B. Wright, eds. *A Zulu King Speaks.* Pietermaritzburg: University of Natal Press, 1987.

Weber, Max. "Politics as a Vocation." In *From Max Weber: Essays in Sociology*. Edited by H. H. Gerth and C. Wright Mills. New York: Oxford University Press, 1946.

———. *The Theory of Social and Economic Organization*. New York: Free Press, 1957.

Weinrich, A. K. H. *Chiefs and Councils in Rhodesia*. London: Heinemann, 1971.

Welsh, David. "The Growth of Towns." In *The Oxford History of South Africa*. Vol. 2. Edited by Monica Wilson and Leonard Thompson. London: Oxford University Press, 1971.

Wentzel, Marie. "Historical Origins of Hostels in South Africa: Migrant Labour and Compounds." In *Communities in Isolation: Perspectives on Hostels in South Africa*, edited by Anthony Minnaar. Pretoria: Human Sciences Research Council, 1993.

Wolpe, Harold. "Capitalism and Cheap Labour-Power." *Economy and Society* 1, no. 4 (1972).

Woods, Gavin. "Hostel Residents—A Socio-Psychological and Humanistic Perspective." In *Communities in Isolation: Perspectives on Hostels in South Africa*, edited by Anthony Minnaar. Pretoria: Human Sciences Research Council, 1993.

Worden, Nigel. *The Making of Modern South Africa*. Oxford: Blackwell, 1994.

Wright, John. "Politics, Ideology, and the Invention of the Nguni." In *Resistance and Ideology in Settler Societies*, edited by Tom Lodge. Johannesburg: Ravan Press, 1986.

Wright, John, and Carolyn Hamilton. "Traditions and Transformations." In *Natal and Zululand from Earliest Times to 1910*, edited by Andrew Duminy and Bill Guest. Pietermaritzburg: University of Natal Press, 1989.

Zizek, Slavoj. *The Sublime Object of Ideology*. New York: Verso, 1989.

Zulu, Paulus M. "An Identification of Base-Line Socio-Political Structures in Rural Areas, Their Operation and Potential Role in Community Development in KwaZulu." University of Zululand Occasional Paper (1984).

———. "The Rural Crisis: Authority Structures and Their Role in Development." In *Up Against the Fences: Poverty, Passes and Privilege in South Africa*, edited by Hermann Giliomee and Lawrence Schlemmer. Cape Town: David Philip, 1985.

Index

Adam, Heribert, 61
Adult Education Consultants, 47, 50
AEC. *See* Adult Education Consultants
African National Congress, 26, 38, 46, 48,
51–53, 70, 76, 78; and African
nationalism, 97–98; and Buthelezi,
Mangosuthu, 61, 64; and chiefs, 30,
63–69, 73, 76–79, 82–83, 96–102; and
CODESA, 83; and CONTRALESA, 66,
71, 77–78; and democracy, 26, 82,
97–98; and IFP, 76, 86, 88, 100; and
indirect rule, 30, 101; and Inkatha, 43,
50, 60–61, 64; and land restitution, 99;
and modernism, 63, 98; Morogoro
Conference, 64; and nonracialism, 26,
31, 60, 97; and separate development,
63–64, 68; and socialism, 98; and
"traditional weapons," 88; and
traditionalism, 56, 98; Youth League,
31, 61; and Zwelithini, Goodwill, 76
African nationalism, 30–31; and ANC,
97–98; and Buthelezi, Mangosuthu,
58–59, 61–62; and Inkatha, 60–62; and
separate development, 32–33, 56. *See
also* Black Consciousness
African Renaissance, 98
Afrikaner Resistance Movement, 70–71
Afrikaner Volksfront, 85
Alexandra, 53, 115n87
All African Convention, 29, 109n64
Althusser, Louis: and historical
materialism, 8; and ideology, 8–12, 18
Ama-Afrika, 43, 47, 50
ANC. *See* African National Congress
Anglo-American Corporation, 61
anthropology, 2, 14–15, 18, 25, 72, 94,
107n36
apartheid: and ethnicity, 39; and indirect
rule, 15, 77; opposition to, 32, 38, 45,
49–50, 59–60, 64, 66, 78, 82; origins of,
22; and urban demarcation, 86. *See also*
separate development
Apter, David, 56
Arendt, Hannah, 80–81
A-Team, 43, 46
authority, 79–83
AWB. *See* Afrikaner Resistance Movement
Azanian People's Organization, 70–71
AZAPO. *See* Azanian People's
Organization

Badenhorst, Rudolf, 47
Bantu Authorities Act (1951), 24–27,
32–33, 36, 63, 94; and chiefs, 24–27;
and democracy, 26
Bantustans. *See* separate development
Barayi, Elijah, 51
Basson, Nico, 44, 50, 52
Beaufre, Andre, 44
Bekhuzulu, Cyprian, 26–27, 61
Berlin Conference (1884), 2
Biko, Steven, 59, 61
Black Consciousness, 58–59, 61
"black-on-black violence," 44
Bophuthatswana, 33
BOSS. *See* Bureau of State Security
Botha, Louis, 13–14, 18, 106n54
Botha, P. W., 44, 51
Brookes, Edgar, 3, 12
Bundy, Colin, 29
Bureau of State Security, 49, 58
Buthelezi Commission, 62
Buthelezi, Mangosuthu Gatsha: and
African nationalism, 58–59, 61–62; and
ANC, 61, 64; and Biko, Steven, 61; and
Black Consciousness, 58–59, 61; and

Rochester Studies in
African History and the Diaspora

Lightning Source UK Ltd.
Milton Keynes UK
UKHW010233291122
413003UK00003B/25